Lemuria

The Buried Truth

By: Tiffany Wardle

Table of Contents

PREFACE

Can you imagine living for thousands of years in beautiful surroundings during a time of peace? Would you like to live in a place described as 'heaven on earth'? Have you ever felt that you do not belong or that you struggle to fit in? The Lemurians know these feelings well...

The secret tale of Lemuria is no longer my secret to keep. This catalogue of events has been buried within me for years. It is now time to tell the tale of Lemuria. This book may unlock a memory within you about your ancestry in Lemuria. These facts may already live in your subconscious. The truth is that many of us may already know the tale deep down, as the Lemurian history already lies in our DNA.

The existence of Lemurians has been debated for centuries. Edgar Cayce and Einstein touched on theories of our magical cousins. Some people have documented that the Lemurian race still exist among us. Tales have been told about hidden, surviving Lemurians living within mountains and under seas. Are any of these stories true? This is for you to decide.

Lemurian roots are awakening again. There is a fire within some of the bellies of true believers, a fire that will spread, the same way the fire spread on the motherland Lemuria thousands of years ago. The flames on the motherland Lemuria (also fondly known as Mu), may have been put out, but the fire still burns in some of our hearts. The more we ignite the flame within, the more the memories will come flooding back.

Here is a beautiful yet tragic tale of the mystical people of Lemuria. The memories are my own. They are memories that I found buried within my soul. These memories describe a heavenly land and a bloody war: a beautiful contradiction.

It is said that the motherland Lemuria sunk and is now buried in the Pacific Ocean. However, the story is far from dead. Even though the Lemurian continent is buried beneath the waves, can we keep the memories alive?

HISTORY: LIFE IN LEMURIA

If you were told that the Lemurians lived on this planet for fifty thousand years, would you believe it? Have you ever wondered why you are here or where you came from? Do you ever think about Atlantis and the tale of the lost city? Are you able to comprehend a story about fifth-dimensional, telepathic, magical, eight-foot-tall beings that inhabited this Earth with a lifespan far greater than we can imagine?

It is said that Atlantis reigned for a mere twelve thousand years. So, how do we know more about the Atlanteans than the Lemurians who reigned for over fifty thousand years? It is as if the Lemurians wanted their continent kept secret, until now.

It has been written that the people of Lemuria seemed the more superior race of the two and were here way before Atlantis was ever thought about. It is said that the continent of Lemuria spread from the Californian coast line, across the Indian Ocean, Easter Islands, Fiji Islands and Japan.

The majority of Lemurians had long blond hair and blue eyes. Their clothes were plain, modest and simple, yet they wore finery to ceremonies for their priests and their gods. They were mainly telepathic beings at first, only learning to speak when they began conversing with other races.

Lemurians had a uniqueness to them, as they were all very psychic beings. Their capacity to manifest all they needed was unprecedented. Living without ego, they did not need many material possessions. They were a happy, peaceful and content race. The Lemurian race could allegedly create miracles at the blink of their third, magical eye. This beautiful race believed in love, equality and looking after everything within the land of Mu. They also believed in a simple, sacred life. It was a place where people could live in the moment without worrying for the future. There was never any anxiety regarding money, food or home.

These sacred people lived in communities without fear. Why would they know fear? They knew only love. The word love was widely used, not just for close families but for everyone. The 'Love Thy Neighbour' concept was used way before the Bible stated it. The Lemurian people loved each other like brother and sister. Life was heavenly, full of love and trust.

The difference between the modern world and the life in Lemuria is vast. We modern humans are more fearful, ego-led people. Can you imagine a life without fear? A life without need? A life where manifesting your every need is possible? A life likened to heaven on earth? A life of good health? This was how the Lemurians lived, full of love for each other. That is, until it all changed when Atlantis came along.

CHAPTER ONE

The Story of Rochelle: The Introduction of an Angel

Rochelle is an angel of Lemuria and Atlantis. Rochelle has a prolific story that could change the lives of many. There are so many humans who will resonate with this tale so, for your sake, the story is shared.

The flames were getting closer and closer to the towns. Rochelle knew it was time to act, and fast. With all her angelic might, she created a hazy mist of calm over the Lemurians that were about to sink with the waves or go down with the flames. The mist created a calmness that took over the townspeople.

This is Rochelle's most vivid yet horrifying memory of Lemuria. However, this angelic being has a lot to share with you, so she will start from the very beginning for you.

Rochelle was not the only angel within the land of Mu, or Lemuria as you may call it. There were also angels guiding Lemurians. There were angelic beings within the congress and within the priesthood. Some angels would advise the priestesses and some were often found conversing with the elders of Lemuria and prophesying the future of the Motherland. Rochelle loved all of her angelic friends. Rochelle and the other angels were forever warning the people of Lemuria about the future atrocity: the fall of Lemuria.

Rochelle often held angelic counsel within Lemuria. Rochelle would speak to Adama, the main priest of Lemuria. She would also speak with Zadiel, the old wise soul and community priest of Mu.

The archangels Ariel and Jophiel joined in the counsel. These angels of the highest angelic realms would help the townsfolk and the elders, offering advice to anyone who could see or sense them.

Rochelle was a statuesque, flame-haired beauty. Rochelle and the angels held daily counsel with twelve priests and priestesses. During this sacred ceremony, Rochelle would beg the Lemurians to move on, because they knew great storms were coming. The angels knew the gods would be displeased with the Lemurians if they carried on warring with the people of Atlantis. Rochelle knew the gods would destroy the whole continent. Archangel Metatron would often head up the counsel, insisting that the Lemurians must stop this talk of war with the newer, younger rivalling continent of Atlantis. Metatron would explain in great detail that the land of Mu was going to sink during great storms. This would horrify the peaceful, loving and loyal Lemurians, so they needed to set sail to new horizons.

Rochelle started to notice the priests and priestesses of Lemuria were becoming more and more agitated with the people of Atlantis. Lemurians communicated peacefully, while the Atlanteans did not. Lemurians treated all people of all ranks equally and the people of Atlantis would not. The people of Atlantis were starting to demonstrate signs of egocentrism and this was bordering on a dictatorial existence. The Lemurians had been passive for so many years, yet now they were completely overcome with worry, as they were unsure of the actions of the Atlanteans. Lemuria was such a peaceful place so this new emotion called 'worry' was unheard of. Things were quickly changing in Lemuria and Rochelle was not the only one who noticed it.

Rochelle would often be present when the priests of Lemuria talked of the issues with Atlantis. The elders and the priests spoke for many months about how to handle the unusual turn of events. Of course, they wanted to make peace with Atlantis. They worried that the people of Lemuria would see the greed in Atlantis and be lured into this excessive way of life. The priests of Mu however, still wanted to have faith in their people. The priests believed that the Lemurian community would still crave the more simplistic way of life. However, the priests were   intelligent beings that did not leave much to chance and wanted to control potential dangers to their race.

Rochelle overheard the priests talking, they had decided to sail over the seas to Atlantis to hold counsel with the Atlanteans. The Lemurians put this to the Atlanteans and were welcomed across to their land. It was time for the red-headed angel Rochelle, to stage an angelic intervention.

CHAPTER TWO

The Story of Rochelle Continued

After a long journey over to Atlantis, five priests, the King and Rochelle were weary from living on the ship. However, they were to go straight to counsel with Atlantis. Only some in Atlantis would have the power to see this flame-haired, stunning angel. Not everyone possessed this spiritual gift.

The Lemurians were welcomed kindly by the Atlanteans. Rochelle noticed the King of Atlantis was in full gold-threaded robes and meant business. The King looked right at the angel, so Rochelle knew he was aware of her presence. When the Lemurians departed the ships they were embraced by the all-powerful Atlantean King. They were then greeted by some priests of Atlantis and head Atlantean naval officers. Rochelle knew that this polite, warm, Atlantis welcome was not authentic. Rochelle could sense they had tricks up their royal sleeves.

The Atlanteans were keen to show the Lemurians what they had been working on. The people of Atlantis tried to wow them with their modern technology, loudly boasting as they walked along their shore lines to show them their boats and their latest naval designs. All the Atlantean officers now seemed to acknowledge the tall, beautiful angel. It was clear the Atlanteans possessed the psychic skills needed to see angels. Rochelle was almost impressed with the Atlanteans. The Lemurians were shown around the industrial site that the Atlanteans were so proud of. The priests of Lemuria looked on pleasantly at everything the Atlanteans had done. The workers on the docks were very skilled, hard labourers, and the structures were all well thought out. The processes were cleverly mastered and intelligently designed. The hierarchy in Atlantis was clear for all to see.

The Lemurians looked on in wonder, but deep down they knew this hierarchical structure would not work in the long run. They knew this because their gift of forethought was far greater than that of the Atlanteans. Lemurians had the foresight to predict how a hierarchy could undermine people. They knew this would affect the lower-calibre workers in hundreds of years, if not sooner, and would cause a future of suppression. The Lemurians had more futuristic skills than those of Atlantis. The people of Mu had built a contemporary, peaceful continent that had successfully worked for thousands of years. The Atlanteans were considered newborns in comparison. 'How could they possibly know what they were doing?' Rochelle thought to herself.

Rochelle smiled and nodded with the rest of the Lemurians. Her piercing, sky-blue, watchful eye concluded that the two belief systems were never going to collaborate.

The Lemurian King and Rochelle were reading each other's thoughts telepathically, while the counsel of Atlantis boasted about new technologies.

Adama, a head Priest of Lemuria, spoke up, 'I can understand that newer ships and futuristic technology can ease the crossing of the seas. However, do you not think that these hierarchies you have created will encourage competition between men, leading them to temptation and the creation of the ego?'

It was clear that Adama could not listen to them anymore. The rest of the Lemurians nodded politely, not wanting to agitate their neighbours. Reading the minds of the Atlanteans, Rochelle knew they were angered by Adama's outburst.

The Atlanteans continued walking them along the shores of their vast land. The ocean there had a very different feel than that of the Lemurian Sea. The beautiful blue stretch of water felt powerful and hungry to command, like a jealous prince awaiting his father's crown. Rochelle looked out at the serene turquoise ocean in wonder of what lay beneath. One day would Atlantis also be buried under this vast ocean? The Atlanteans continued to happily boast, displaying their new boats, saying how they were more than capable of ruling their own continent. This appeared arrogant and superficial to the Lemurians, but they all managed to stay composed and neutral during the visit - except for Adama.

The Lemurians and the angel were evidently not only there to observe the lay of the land but to get a psychic sense of the people. Psychically reading the energy of the community, would give them a greater idea of this newer race and their future plans for domination. Rochelle had her own premonitions on this matter and they were not positive ones.

CHAPTER THREE

Damien's Story: The Warrior's Tale

A tall, handsome, blond warrior wearing tremendous leather armour appeared from the Lemurian coastline, carrying a sword like a true soldier. His pale skin and blue eyes looked weary from warrior practice. His enormous presence filled the entire beach. His aura was strong; it was clear that he was a warrior who would die for his country.

Damien was his name.

Although Damien may have looked young to you, say twenty-four years of age, his body was over one thousand years old. Damien was still considered a young Lemurian. This is difficult for modern day humans to understand, as they do not live as long as Lemurians.

Every one hundred years or so, Damien looked slightly older. Adama, the priest, looked forty-five years old, and was considered an elder. He looked old and wise to Damien.

Damien was born to be active. He loved being busy and exuded much energy. Damien was also born to protect his beloved country - the motherland. Damien could not explain the love he felt for the land of Mu. It was a heavenly feeling that Damien wanted and needed to preserve. Damien knew he was a warrior from a young age, bred to protect. All Lemurians would rather participate in a peaceful protest than a war, as they were a peaceful race, but times were changing and they knew war would soon be upon them. So Damien knew he had to be prepared to fight. When the rumour mill began about war and Atlantis, Damien felt his calling.

Damien practiced the art of war daily. His friends would all play fight with each other and all were well equipped for battle. They were ready and they believed unanimously that they would win the war. They all thought it would be easy, but they were wrong.

They had all heard tales about this new continent called Atlantis. This was the reason that warriors, such as Damien, were being trained. Lemurians had all lived so peacefully in the past, but Damien knew deep down that this peace would one day be replaced with a battle and that warriors would be needed to defend their country and the people of Mu.

Damien knew only of hearsay from the townsfolk about a war. He had heard tales about Atlantis from the worried townsmen. Local folk were becoming unnerved by the fearmongering. Emotions such as fear and worry became prominent and yet these emotions were previously unknown to them all.

The young warriors thought they were the kings of battle. They loved to sit and talk about strategies of war with Atlantis. Charlie was Damien's dearest friend. With darker hair and a stature of six feet tall, Charlie differed from the majority of soldiers. Most soldiers were at least eight feet tall with light hair and lighter eyes. Charlie's darker features were unusual: his face was unique because of his dark, distinguished eyes. He was excitable about the battle and would talk about it for hours. Charlie's mother was always telling him to calm down about war but he refused. He felt it was his duty to protect his country, the motherland, and that is what he would do.

The warrior friends would sit for hours in the fields talking about swords and armour, teaching each other the latest skills. They were happy in their naivety.

In contrast, the elders would often walk around the markets talking calmly as the warrior boys practiced their fighting skills. The elders, like the priest Adama, were well-respected and admired. However, the warriors knew the priests held secrets about a visit to Atlantis, an invasion; they knew the elders kept secrets and surreptitious information that was undisclosed to mere townsfolk.

As they playfully fought, the warrior boys talked of this secret trip to Atlantis that they had heard about. The trip across the ocean was soon becoming common knowledge to all people. The townsfolk all believed that the priests and the elders should acknowledge the trip and tell of their findings in Atlantis, as the common people were becoming nervous.

Why did Damien feel nervous? He thought to himself; he was a warrior; he should not feel fear. The Lemurians had everything they ever needed and wanted in Lemuria. The people of Mu never feared the unknown. Damien became unnerved. This was a new feeling for Damien. Times were changing.

As the warriors skilfully fought each other near the markets, Damien could clearly sense the emotions of the local people.

Damien heard whispers in the air as Adama walked by. He heard whispers through the market like: 'We have been such a peaceful community for so long; could we not maintain the contentment and leave Atlantis alone?'

It was as if Damien could hear the people's thoughts. If the elders remained tight lipped about the secret visit and the proceedings, they would all have to draw their own conclusions.

Damien assumed the elders would discourage Atlantis and put a stop to the rivalry. Otherwise, if they did not leave Lemuria well alone, the Lemurian warriors would fight them, destroy them and win! 'Of course we will win', they all naively thought.

Damien began play fighting with Charlie using a new silver sword. It felt heavy, which slowed his feet. Charlie swiped straight at Damien's chest and missed, so Damien pretended to strike him in the throat and won. The battle was swift and it was over. They laughed and onlookers amused themselves at Charlie's defeat. Charlie took it well as Damien always seemed to win.

As the warrior boys hugged like gentleman, they noticed a group of market people huddling together close by. They walked over to the crowds.

A speech was being set up in the square. A traditional sacrifice began as they neared the front of the crowds. A white goat lay dead, bleeding in front of them. This was offered to the gods. Damien looked up to the heavens and prayed. Damien knew that at that moment the gods were listening and Damien felt loved by them. A sacred blessing began so they fell to their knees. They all openly prayed with their own usual prayer. Then Damien saw Zadiel, the priest of the community, standing tall. Zadiel's long, shaggy light brown hair and beard made him stand out from the crowd. He wore his golden armour and red cloak to address the people. Zadiel began to speak to the masses in his usual empowering and confident manner.

The townsfolk were told they were the greater continent and that the Lemurian traditions would not be overthrown. Zadiel was calm but strong. His booming voice carried over the crowds effortlessly. The depth of his voice said 'I am a true ruler' and so they all felt safe.

Zadiel said, 'We will stand together as Lemurians. We give thanks to our gods for giving us courage in times like these. We are as one with our motherland and our gods, and we stay as one.'

Damien felt these words so strongly that he cheered. The noise coming from him was more like an animalistic growl than a human cheer.

Damien believed in Zadiel's words from the pit of his stomach and was happy to fight for his people if need be. Damien felt pleased to be a Lemurian that day and he knew he was in capable hands.

Damien left the speech excitable and full of testosterone, knowing they would be going into battle to do nothing but win! Damien slept well that night.

CHAPTER FOUR

Charlie's Story: The Warriors Unite

Charlie had all his weapons ready and was excited to be by the side of his best friend, Damien. They were about to meet their new commander and Charlie could not wait. Charlie knew they would lead this battle and win this war within two sunsets. Charlie knew they would then be coming home victoriously, back to his beloved land.

Charlie picked up his heavy weapons and followed the others. They all walked in single file to the ocean's edge to meet fellow warriors. The sun was rising above the ocean. It was as if the sun was telling them to rise as warriors. The scene was beautiful and calm, which was a huge contrast to the way Charlie was feeling inside.

Charlie was finally greeted by his new commander and the new team of warriors. As Charlie scoured the ranks, he realised the men standing on the sand were exceptionally well-trained warriors. Charlie may have a lot more to learn than he thought. Although this was a knock to his ego, he stayed optimistic. Charlie was partnered with the new commander and started immediately. He always learned quickly, mastering new sword techniques. One by one, they were taught by the commander himself. He stood over eight and a half feet tall. He was stronger than any other warrior Charlie had met before. Charlie was pleased to be under his command. Charlie listened carefully and acted precisely because he wanted to defend his country with honour.

The warriors practiced day and night. Charlie learned so much within such a short space of time, because they needed to defend Lemuria and show that they were the older, more mature, superior race.

The commander was called Thesis. He was a great warrior and kin of one of the elders. An elder is one of the oldest living Lemurians and, because Thesis was a blood relative of an elder, the warriors believed him to be wise beyond his years. His wisdom was to be respected. He did not hold back on knowledge nor did he patronise anyone who showed ignorance in any way. Thesis was a true Lemurian, modeling meritocracy within his teachings.

The warriors felt safe with Thesis and they quickly bonded like family. They were all told of plans to make progress over the following days. They set up a camp and slept outside under the stars and they felt peace. Damien and Charlie both had a funny feeling that this was the calm before the storm.

CHAPTER FIVE

Damien and the Winds of Change

As Damien lay under the stars, he saw a flicker from the distance. It was the elders riding toward the warrior camp, wanting to speak to Thesis. Damien quickly stood up and dressed for the unexpected visit of the elders. He sensed there was news and awaited their command. This was serious, this could mean war.

The elders were whispering with Thesis and emotions were heightened. The energy had changed; that was very easy for even the most non-psychic Lemurian to see. A frenzied atmosphere commenced between the elders and Thesis. The other soldiers started to awaken; they could smell the tension in the air. Damien quickly got up and picked up his sword. Damien was ready for battle, just in case. As a soldier, being ready for battle was ingrained in his soul. Damien did not think twice about fighting for his country. Emotions and thoughts would not get in the way of protecting the motherland.

As Damien stood ready, he remembered his premonition the night before...

Although he did not like to think of himself as a very psychic Lemurian, Damien had his own gift - the gift of insight, you may call this 'clairvoyance'. Others could speak and feel predictions. Damien could not switch this on like a tap, the insights were not available for him to use all of the time. His gift of insight was more like a series of visions strung together, but this would only happen very occasionally. Damien could not always make sense of these flashes of clairvoyance, but he learned to live with this strange feeling. He was too embarrassed to tell his friends about his premonitions. He was a warrior, not a wizard!

At any given moment, colours would blur his vision, which meant a premonition was coming. This started to happen a few hours before the elders turned up.

Damien could see blurred visions in the black of night. He was staring at the stars and could clearly see Charlie settling to sleep. Then, all of a sudden, Damien heard horses galloping. No one else could hear or see them.

His vision continued and Damien could feel heat and saw yellow in the sky – this yellow was the colour of burning flames! His visions then showed him horses pounding toward the warrior camp with the fires burning all of Lemuria in the background.

Damien's visions then showed him Thesis shouting for the warriors to get up, as they had been invaded!

It turns out Damien's visions were correct. The visitation to Atlantis was not the peaceful protest the elders professed it to be. When Adama, the King and some other priests sailed to Atlantis, the Atlanteans felt threatened by the elders' condescending tones and this had enraged the people of Atlantis. War was upon Lemuria.

Damien blinked his eyes and came out of his psychic state. He was now fully back to the present moment and his visions had gone. Before he knew it, all the warriors were all on their feet. He felt like he had been hypnotised for hours, however his visions had only lasted a matter of moments.

The energy was suddenly electric. The testosterone building up inside them all was like it never had been before. Damien had never felt such a surge of raw energy. He felt like a wild animal ready to pounce, regardless of his safety.

Damien could feel his need to protect as adrenaline took over within this young, inexperienced warrior. Damien's eyes widened as the flames in the background seemed to fly through the air and back down again. Damien then heard the screams. He saw women and children fleeing the central lands.

There were priestesses heading for the long boats, trying to encourage the men to steer the boats. People were running and screaming all over the town. Most of the men wanted to stay and fight. They were angry, as their land had been intentionally invaded without any warning by people who they thought of as vagrants. The Atlanteans had attacked; they had started this unfair, one-sided war. Damien and the other warriors would fight for their country and would not back down.

Damien's eyes were wide with anger and fear. Damien did spare a thought for his family, his young brother, but mostly he wanted to fight; he wanted revenge. He realized how territorial the warriors were as a unit.

This was not a time to look at strategy, to laugh or to play with swords; this was real, raw, gritty war. They were ready.

****

Damien only vaguely remembered what happened next...

They went into battle and straight away someone was slain. His friend Garland lay in front of him - dead. This enraged a sudden fury within him. Damien was disorientated from that moment on. He could hear screams from women, but could hardly see anything, as it was pitch black. The sun was not going to come up for an hour or so. Until then, Damien could not see what he was doing. The one thing Damien didn't know about battle was how tired it made him. His sword was heavy, the armour was weighty and Damien was constantly running to defend himself and the innocent townspeople. Although running on pure adrenaline was easy, his mind soon became weary.

Many men tried to fight and many were killed. Men were killed in their beds as some did not want battle. Some were killed while merely looking out for their family, their land and their community. This was not their war! They were mere townsfolk! Damien was furious as he watched the chaos.

The people of Atlantis did not discuss any of this vengeful attack; this was not a fair fight from the outset. The anger did not stop rising within the young warrior.

The battle ended as quickly as it began. It seemed too fast; it was not what Damien thought it would be - the Lemurians just did not have a chance. The sun started to rise and within an instant the Atlanteans were gone in their boats. Although the Lemurians chased them, the Atlanteans also had magical powers. The warriors from Atlantis were seen fleeing to the shore line and within an instant they were out at sea; it was as if they could bend time. The people of Lemuria looked stunned. They were not used to chaos, but conformity.

In his clairvoyant eye, Damien could see they would be back. He knew the Atlantis warriors would return, again unannounced. Damien knew there would be another visit that could kill many. Damien also felt psychically that they were not here just to create war, the Atlanteans were not here just to attack. Damien wondered what they came for.

The aftermath of the battle was horrific. This was something that Damien had difficulty explaining, not just because he was exhausted, but also because of the blood and the numerous dead bodies left to clear. There were so many children, women and men walking around, lost, many of them with a look of sheer terror on their faces. The enormity of the devastation was incomprehensible. The battle was so brief. How was the Lemurian community destroyed so quickly? The beautiful, blue sky had turned red with the flames as their heavenly continent was on fire. It was as if heaven had been turned into hell. It was as if the sky was speaking to Damien. The blue calm sky was no more; the red angry atmosphere was now the very air they would breathe.

Damien was angry. He wanted revenge.

Warriors were already plotting and seeking revenge while they carried the dead bodies over to the sacred burial ground. Damien could feel the anger rising within the people. Negative emotion started to spread like an epidemic, a contrast to the usual peaceful Lemurian exteriors. As resentment grew like an open wound, within five to ten minutes a new plague had begun - the plague of fury.

Damien knew he had a choice now. His clairvoyance and his higher spiritual self tried to make him think peacefully. However, his emotions were saying retribution.

Damien seemed to have an angel on his shoulder in times of trouble, an old friend he hadn't seen for years. It was Rochelle.

****

Damien saw Rochelle for the first time when he was a little boy. Damien remembered his little brother was in trouble by the water mills. They had been playing carelessly by the lakes and they became dangerously close to the working mills. Rochelle, his angel, started to whisper in his ear to keep Petrius, his brother, away from the enormous mill turbines. Damien was not looking, not watching Petrius, as he was too busy kicking up the flowers in the field. Rochelle was there again saying, 'Damien look to Petrius, it's time to move now.'

There was something in her voice that made Damien look up. Petrius was dangerously close to edge of the mill, about to fall into the deep and freezing waters. Damien started to run and then realised how far away the mill was from him so Damien called his name: 'Petrius!'

Rochelle shouted 'no, don't call him'. But Damien called his name anyway.

Petrius turned to his big brother, looked startled and fell. This was why Rochelle told Damien not to call the young lad.

Petrius was splashing around in the water, panic stricken and unable to paddle out, as there was no space to swim. The water was freezing cold and very deep, and Damien could see from his face he was too astonished to figure out what to do next.

Damien's brother was not like him, Petrius was a soft soul, a caring and creative young man. Damien was a warrior, an action man. Damien loved play fighting and boisterous acts but his brother preferred the arts, music and creativity. Petrius' forte was never going to be climbing out of an ice cold water mill with a moving turbine near his feet while having the body strength to pull himself over the side.

Rochelle talked Damien through how to get him out and somehow he had more courage and more strength than he'd ever had before. Damien immediately grappled at his brother's clothes and somehow heaved Petrius over the edge. Petrius was coughing and spluttering and was turning blue from the chill. However, Rochelle gave clear and calm instructions to remove the wet clothes and give Damien's over-clothes to Petrius. Rochelle told Damien to turn around and he saw a fire burning near the mill entrance. Damien had not seen this fire before and he strongly believed that Rochelle magically created the fire, but Damien had no proof of that. He was learning that when it came to angels, you just have to trust in what they tell you.

Damien lay his brother near the fire. Petrius looked at Damien, smiled and made a joke. The disaster was over.

Damien learned two things from that day: Firstly, he would always be a protector. Secondly, he had a guardian angel.

****

Damien could not quite believe that he was now a fully grown man standing in the aftermath of a horrendous war and Rochelle was there again. Damien had forgotten about his intense, psychic ability from that dreadful day by the mills. It was such a long time ago that he had moved on and become more of a warrior and less spiritual. Damien could feel Rochelle clearly warning him against his temper and reminding the young warrior to look at the situation through his psychic eye. Damien believed wholly that his psychic ability was real, he just didn't want it anymore. He ignored it. Damien was not a little boy anymore, he was a warrior and his whole being was enraged. Damien was hungry for blood. He wanted action and adventure, not meditation and stillness, while his third eye saw the future and spoke to angels. Damien could also never tell the other warriors of his visions. The other warriors would surely laugh at him. Sacred powers were for the intellectuals, the elders and the women, not for boisterous warriors.

Then Damien remembered again about his brother at the mill and he stopped dead still among the chaos all around him.

'Damien!' Rochelle called him over to some woodland, away from the noise. Somehow he knew to follow. Damien felt as if there was an angelic pull, taking him away from the chaos. He felt a magnetic push that made him move over to a wooded area that had not been effected by the war. He was moving further away from the flames. It was as if Rochelle was trying to change his location and his state of mind from fiery to serene. Once he had followed her to the edge of the serene forest, Rochelle immediately calmed him down.

Rochelle said: 'Damien, do not be led by your rage. Your anger for your territory is a lower-based emotion. You do not have to follow the aggressive crowd. You were born with a special gift - the gift of insight. You know you can see ahead, you can see the future and you are skilled in talking to and seeing angels effortlessly. Others practice for years to see angels but you do it so well and so naturally. The angels need someone to channel through, someone who sees them easily, someone who does not force angelic insight. They need a natural talent, a talent who will not read too much into psychic messages, but who can draw from the messages naturally. That person is you, Damien.'

They stood at the edge of the forest while Damien listened to the wind in the trees, whispering like Rochelle's voice in his ears.

Rochelle appeared to Damien strongly now, with her feminine, tall physique and her red hair piled up on top of her head. She was pleading with him in a very loving way.

Rochelle said, 'We asked your parents before you were born if we could borrow you for a special mission and they humbly agreed. We spoke to you before you were born and asked if you would be willing to take on a mission, as your soul was right for us. You were to be born at the correct time for the mission. You have the correct temperament and wisdom within your soul that we need and astrologically we made sure you were born under the perfect moon for the mission. So Damien, all the elements pointed to you. You have ignored your gift for so long that you believe it is not there. However, it is time for you to take your power back.'

Her energy filled him with love and compassion. Damien could almost see the anger within him dissipate like steam rising up from the marsh lands around them.

Rochelle continued, 'Now that you see the chaos around you, you have two choices. You can join in the war and be one of the many, or you can use your god-given gift and rise above.'

Damien: replied, 'I want to rise above. I will obey you to save my people. I want to serve and fight, but I will listen to you as fighting has not got us very far.'

Rochelle said, 'We need your approval so we can continue. I need you to talk to the people. You have the strength to get people to listen to you. You have a warmth in your heart that will make people sympathise with your mission and I know they will listen to you. We need you to help bring talk of revenge to an end. This is not the Lemurian way. There are masses of people that will go against the elders' wishes of peace. The elders will be in counsel now with the angels, priests, priestesses and the King. Damien, I must inform you that the archangels Michael, Metatron, Jophiel and Ariel, will be revealing to the elders once again that Lemuria will fall. The elders will then disclose the information to the masses, wanting to help them, but they will not listen! They will stop trusting! However, you have the people's touch, Damien!'

She was pleading in such a way that he could no longer ignore her.

Rochelle concluded, 'You will inadvertently push the masses to leave. People will listen to you. You will speak the words I give to you. I will be providing you with information. You can tell the people there is an angel on your shoulder. If you wish, you can describe me. I will show my skills to some of the crowd, so that even if they can't see me they will believe you. I will be your guardian angel. I will tell you what to say. I am your guide. I am only here to serve and I am here to help. You must fully trust in me and must follow my exact instructions. This is why it must be you and no other. You are very precise when it comes to receiving instructions. Now, we must start practicing.'

So, Rochelle took him deep into the forest and showed Damien how to see her more clearly. Damien could only see her in times of trouble. However, Rochelle said there was a skill he should learn so Damien could see her vividly at all times. It seemed like she was preparing him for a bigger mission than just talking to a crowd. He could only wonder what it was.

Rochelle magically made a fire and made him concentrate on the flames. The angel said Damien should focus on the flames to keep his mind still. This felt ironic. Again, Damien was staring at flames but this time for good and not for war. She showed him how to stop his mind from wandering. She taught him to meditate. She told him of a meadow Damien must go to in his mind in case his concentration drifts off. Damien didn't understand why he had to go to a meadow in an imaginary world, but Rochelle taught him that if he went to the imaginary meadow in his mind, she would meet him there. She said Damien needed to stay on course and the more he practiced, the easier it would be to connect with her.

Rochelle told him they were running out of time. She said she had one final thing to teach him. Rochelle said Damien must also learn how to raise his vibration. Damien had no idea what she meant. She said that the Lemurians had a very high frequency. Not all Lemurians could see angels, but they could if they 'raised' their energy.

Rochelle said Lemurians were highly evolved beings. They were calm and content and used their minds for the greater good. She told him how they felt inner peace and inner contentment. However, they were all different. Some Lemurians were exceptionally good at manifestation: seeing in their mind exactly what they wanted and then immediately receiving it. However, some Lemurians were better at predicting the future. Rochelle said that he had the power of prediction. She told Damien he was special because he was able to see the guides who give him the messages and the predictions.

Damien was embarrassed with her constant complimentary conversation and his mind started to wander. As his eyes started to glance around the forest, Damien watched the trees and saw an animal moving in the distance. It was a lonely stag in the forest. Damien could almost feel what this stag was thinking. He suddenly felt more at peace and at one with the forest. Damien stared at the beauty of the stag, the huge antlers that made this creature unique. This beast had both a regal and mystical presence. The stag stared right back at him and for a moment Damien felt as though they were connected. It was as if the two worlds of animal and man were one in that very moment, similar to the world of angel and man. It made him realise that they were all one, they were all connected. That's the reason why Damien could connect with Rochelle, an angel, as he felt at one with her.

Rochelle proclaimed, 'The time has come for you to speak up!'

Damien was scared, what if no one listened to him? What if the war had made him delusional and Rochelle was not even real? Damien feared that he just needed something to believe in as his people were suffering. Then Damien realised, 'What choice do I have? I either fight a battle that we are clearly losing or I try something new.'

They walked out of the forest and back on to the track to the sea.

His weary, heavy feet followed the long, sandy lane that took them to the ocean. Damien could see people fleeing their houses as the flames licked the sky nearby. He could see one woman screaming for her child. He could see men wounded. Damien could not help but think, 'What is the reason for this chaos, this disaster?' Damien doubted anyone would know. However, he could smell revenge in the flame-covered air.

Damien could see men heading for the boats looking as though they were heading out to sea to find war. He could sense they would head to the Atlantis coast to make the Atlanteans pay for burning the sacred land of Lemuria.

As Rochelle and Damien got close to the hordes of people, they could almost smell the chaos. People's houses were burning and children were crying. Damien started to feel a sense of calm washing over him like the ocean washing away the debris. He looked for a leader, someone to take charge. The elders were nowhere to be found. His senses told him that the priests were plotting, but the common people needed answers now, not talk among counsel! Damien could clearly see crowds were enraged. Their loud thoughts said they were sick of intellectual conversation, pacifying tactics and strategy; they clearly wanted blood.

Damien ran along the shore line, maneuvering his way between screaming children and dead bodies. He noticed some of the long boats, full of revenge-fueled warriors, had already left the shore. Only a few hours before, Damien would have been the first warrior on the boat. He knew now that he was on a different mission.

Damien felt an immense surge of power as Rochelle appeared by his side. This was the closest Damien had ever felt to her. The very quick lesson Rochelle had given him in the forest was paying off. Damien could now feel and see an angel next to him much more clearly than ever before.

He felt safe with Rochelle by his side. Covered in armour, dressed as a royal warrior with a heavy sword, Damien had never felt such protection as he did now from Rochelle. If anyone could see this scene of a soft, angelic, loving being standing so close to this strong, armoured, warrior they would have never believed it. The contradiction was ludicrous. The energy she gave to him was clearly from another realm and this showed him that if he ever wanted to connect with his guardian angel, all he needed was faith and Rochelle would be there.

It was time.

Rochelle nodded and pointed to an area in the square, an opening amongst the chaos. Houses and trees were on fire and chaos presided. However, there seemed to be a circle of calm in the middle of this opening. Damien could not help but feel Rochelle has created a space of serenity.

Rochelle gestured for him to move forward. It was time for her to speak through him. Damien nodded with respect and took centre stage.

CHAPTER SIX

Damien's Story Continued

Damien began to address the crowds: 'People. People of Lemuria, listen!'

The young, inexperienced warrior's hands were sweating. He was standing in a circle of chaos while everyone in front of him ran frantically up and down the hill, wondering where to go for safety. Damien could hardly hear himself above the screams and cries.

'People, listen to me!'

Damien heard that same kind of bellow come out of his mouth all those years ago when he called for his brother.

Some people stopped momentarily, but you could see their anxious faces as they looked on to flee their homes and find their loved ones.

Damien looked down and suddenly there was a barrel on the floor to his right, Damien stood on it. The barrel was not there before; this was the work of an angel. Damien started to wonder if the others could see her too.

Then, something extraordinary happened. Damien could see Rochelle on his left and she looked as if she was blowing the air. Damien could see a blue mist coming from her throat. This blue mist surrounded the crowd in front of them and more and more of the masses stood to attention. Damien did not utter another word and was merely standing on a barrel, yet people were taking notice. Again, this was the work of Rochelle.

People looked dazed yet inquisitive. The blue energy coming from Rochelle's throat looked magical to him. Damien had no idea what she was doing but the anxious young man knew it was his time to speak. The energy coming from Rochelle now turned yellow and more of it started coming out of her stomach area. Then, she aimed this energy right at him.

Suddenly, Damien felt more courageous than he'd ever been, even more so than when he saved his brother. He threw his voice confidently for all to hear. The cries stopped, the angry crowds stopped running and started to pay attention.

Damien: 'Friends, fellow Lemurians. We must work together to save Lemuria. The only way to survive is to work as a team. We must not attack in vengeance; we must stop this! We need to start thinking clearly and plan carefully! This is the only way to keep our families safe. Running for the hills and the ocean is not the answer. This will leave less people to defend when the masses of Atlanteans return; and they will return. They will come back with more warriors and more boats, wanting more battles.

They will think it is easy to attack us. They have succeeded once before. This will fill their empty heads with victory and they will want more.

They were not here on our land just to fight, but to test us and see how spontaneously we could respond. They feel we do not respond quickly enough, as we are less equipped than they are. They feel the need to win. We must stay, we must unite and we must be prepared. Stay here, Lemurians, and let your loved ones find you here. Stay with the masses.'

Without thinking, Damien sat on the floor, just as Rochelle sat down. Damien realised he was a puppet to her requests. He was purely channeling her thoughts and was strangely calm and happy to be her vessel of peace. Damien had received no attention from the crowds; he wanted to fight like the rest of them! However, Damien was going against his will for an angel. Strange, yes, but he knew Rochelle was right. He had no idea if everyone else could see Rochelle; he guessed they could not. Damien had no idea what that strange blue mist was, but he was pleased it worked. He didn't know why she gave him a yellow mist of energy from herself, either, but Damien was pleased to feel as confident as he did to talk to those raging people. It felt as if the colours were representing something. The blue from her throat seemed to represent calm and the yellow from her stomach gave him courage. It felt as if the blue mist aided communication and the yellow mist was for strength.

The main feeling Damien had when channeling Rochelle was confidence. Damien was simply a messenger passing on an important statement. He felt safe knowing that he was channeling a being that had far greater knowledge than all of them. Damien knew the message was for the good of the people. The channeling became easy as he truly trusted his source, Rochelle.

The once-angered crowds now all sat on the floor like peaceful protestors. One by one, people joined them on the terrain, with the orange flames still covering the trees in the forest behind them. There were still many people running down the hill, frantically looking for loved ones and fleeing their houses. As they ran by and saw them all sitting peacefully, they started to join the sitting protest. It was as if there was an invisible chord pulling the fellow Lemurians toward them. The newer masses did not look bewildered; they did not even ask questions. They just came and sat down. Damien could still see the blue haze above their heads. However, they seemed oblivious to this and so he felt they could not see it.

It was truly fascinating. This blue mist could silence a huge crowd in the middle of chaos. How ingenious. Damien would never question Rochelle again. He trusted her and this time he meant it.

Every moment of silence from the sitting crowd was like a badge of honour to Damien. The peaceful protest was going well until they started to feel the pound of horses' hooves on the ground beneath them. This could only mean one thing: the elders were coming.

CHAPTER SEVEN

Damien and Adama

'Better late than never', Damien thought as the elders approached. He could sense the crowds getting agitated as they saw the priests coming. Damien could see Adama coming on his usual stunning, brown stallion. The priest was covered in armour but his long blond hair and demeanor still made him stand out from the crowd. Standing at way over eight feet tall, Adama had an air of such great presence that he could not be missed. Adama got off his horse and came toward them. He did not seem stunned at the peaceful protest they appeared to be having on the ground. He took his helmet off and looked at the crowd. Damien was not sure if Adama saw him as he did not acknowledge Damien at all.

Adama addressed the crowd, 'People of Lemuria. This is a tragedy to our land. We have been invaded by barbarians. We must stick together and defend our territory. We must stand up to those who are against us and our policies.'

Murmurs from the crowd became louder. The crowds were crying out, 'Why should we listen to you?', 'Where were you?', 'Where is my son?', 'I cannot find my family!'

The crowd gave Adama a very different welcome to the one they had given the unknown warrior. The crowd felt their leaders had let them down and they felt disgruntled. The murmurs started to form into questions: 'Why did you have to go to Atlantis? If you had not gone, this would not have happened!'

Adama looked calm and controlled as he addressed them all: 'I see your concerns. Trust that we are on your side. We will find your loved ones. We went to let the Atlanteans know that their forward thinking behavior would run their country into the ground. We were trying to help them. We did not attack them. They have attacked us. Now, we must all stick together.' Adama was trying to get the attention of the masses, but they were drifting off. Some started to get up and Damien could hear grumbles from those who stayed.

Rochelle pushed Damien to stand up.

At first, Damien refused. There was no way he was going to interrupt Adama, a head priest. Adama didn't even know Damien existed.

The last time Adama addressed Damien was when he was a young lad play-fighting with his brother. Damien dropped his wooden sword and Adama picked up the sword and told him it was a good one. Damien ignored his words, not knowing who he was. His father looked a little embarrassed by his son's conduct and bowed to Adama. His father then put his hands on Damien's shoulders and edged back so Adama could pass. Damien did not know what all the fuss was about.

When Adama left, Damien's father scolded him for not being more polite. Damien was wary of Adama from that moment on.

Damien stood forward and Adama looked at him. Rochelle encouraged Damien to speak. To his disbelief, Adama stood back a little and let Damien hold the crowd's attention. Damien could then feel Adama looking over his shoulder and Damien realised that he gave way for Rochelle to speak and not Damien. Adama could see the angel guide.

Damien called out, 'People!' He could hear the bellow coming from his mouth. Rochelle was speaking through him again.

'We must stay with the masses! All of us must stick together to conquer this disruption. Fighting one another is not our mission. We need to remain together as one and look after each other and our land. Remember our tradition, remember our civility. We all love and respect our land, all of us. Let us be respectful now.'

Damien could not understand what was happening, but everyone was listening. People sat back down. Adama, staring at the floor, was nodding encouragingly at his persistence, nodding to everything Damien was saying!

Damien was a nobody! Adama was the head priest! Damien could not believe it, but something in him made him keep his composure.

Rochelle moved forward, stood in front of the crowd and blew out a pink mist from her heart. Damien was getting used to these colours now and knew they all meant something. She walked by Damien and stood with Adama. He was now completely convinced Adama could see Rochelle, as he was looking straight at her. There seemed to be a mutual respect from Adama to Rochelle. The high priest and the angel were unquestionably allies.

The pink mist calmed everyone. People started to smile. Damien could see their thoughts, as his psychic ability was always substantially stronger when he was connected to Rochelle. Damien felt as if Rochelle facilitated his strength and he was now even more connected to the angel. Damien was grateful for her presence.

The pink mist settled and a new, more loving feeling seemed to come over the crowd. Damien gathered that a pink mist encouraged love between the masses. He carried on talking. He spoke of the wonderment of their land and their brotherhood, how the bond between man and the motherland would not be broken. He did not need to say anything else. Everyone was hooked on his words. He liked the pink mist!

It was clear that Damien and Rochelle were a team; her thoughts, her powerful colours and his voice. Damien was needed to assist the masses and she was definitely a necessity to aide control over an angry crowd. He finally knew his role: psychic angel channeler.

The masses grew and grew and then Adama spoke again. This time, everyone listened. Afterwards, they all did the usual sacred prayer and song and they were once again united. An unruly chorus of anger had been silenced by a chorus of song and prayer. Unity and calm prevailed again.

CHAPTER EIGHT

Damien and Adama: The Brotherhood

The masses were instructed by the elders to return to their homes to be with their families. The elders said they would be giving instructions on how they could help with the rebuilding of the land. They were told to forget about the tragedy and to try to look forward. Their job was to remain peaceful. The community left in unison.

Damien stayed.

Adama and other elders were standing in a semi-circle watching the flames in the distance finally simmer down. Damien felt the same ease around Adama that he had felt all those years before as an innocent child. Damien was not expecting the warmth of Adama's presence to extend to him, an unknown. However, Adama turned and looked at Damien with kind eyes. Adama had very big blue eyes that were trusting and seemed wise and all-knowing; they were mesmerising. He was the head priest for a reason. Damien could feel Adama's aura giving off a feeling of pure love, wisdom and peace.

Adama said, 'Thank you' to Damien. Then he embraced Damien like a brother.

Adama then turned to Rochelle, bowed and said, 'Eternally grateful, Rochelle. I give great thanks to you'. He then looked at Damien and beckoned 'come'.

Damien wanted to stay with Rochelle. He needed to ask her what had just happened.

How did a haze of colour come from an angel?

How did Rochelle still a maddened crowd?

Damien knew his duty was to his high priest, so he continued.

Rochelle left them to work.

CHAPTER NINE

Adama's Secret Story

Adama knew that Damien was the chosen one from the time Damien was a young boy. Unbeknownst to Damien, the elders chose this fearless warrior at a young age to stand up and speak to the masses. The elders knew not to intervene with his childhood. As a priest, Adama knew the importance of normality in one's childhood; that was something Adama did not receive himself. Adama's father and the other elders knew thousands of years before that Damien would be the voice of the people. The elders were all capable of making accurate, psychic predictions. The premonitions of these great men informed the elders many years before that there was to be a war. Adama knew that there would be a war and that the masses would lose faith in him, their head priest. He knew that the crowds would listen to a common boy, a voice of the people.

The elders decided in counsel that Rochelle would be sent to the young boy to help grow and nurture his psychic ability.

As a son of the original elders, Adama was forever grateful to his forefathers for creating an abundant land. In Adama's humble opinion, his own father was the wisest of all forefathers. His father always professed that a time would come when there would be war. Walking through the endless fields behind the castle gates, his father would explain that one day a huge war would begin between two great continents, namely Lemuria and Atlantis. His father would talk for hours while they admired the wildlife of the nearby forests, the same forests that were now destroyed by the Atlantean warriors. His father explained that this day would come and that Adama would have to make a choice: war or peace.

Adama was informed by his father that a huge majority of Lemurians would start to believe that Atlantis was the greater continent. They would start to whisper that Atlantis was the better place to be. His father walked for miles in his grey, regal robes telling the young Adama in his authoritative, husky voice that the majority would either want to fight with Atlantis or live with them. Adama was told they could stop this controversy with the help of a young boy who was not born of their bloodline. Adama was informed that this old, wise soul called Damien would be there to help maintain the pure essence of Lemuria.

More recently, Adama knew the predicted day of war was fast approaching when Rochelle came to him. Adama had not seen her privately in many years. Rochelle was often in counsel yes, but did not deal with Adama on a one-to-one basis very often. Hundreds of years before, Rochelle came to him in a dream and told Adama he was not to react when people started to dislike and distrust the head priest. Adama waited years and years for the catastrophe of war to happen. He consulted the elders and prayed to the gods. It took many years for the angel's premonition to take place.

He knew the winds of change were beginning the day they visited Atlantis. Adama could see the glint in the eye of the Atlanteans. Adama could read their malicious energy - it was obvious they were secretly plotting to war with Lemuria. It was clear they wanted to be the ultimate rulers. To become the dominant race, they needed Lemurian secrets. They required a glimpse of the sacred Lemurian land. Adama could tell by their energy that the Atlanteans had a huge desire to use their newfound psychic powers on the elders; they were trying to read the elders' well-trained minds. They wanted knowledge from the Lemurians during the trip to ensure their triumph over Lemuria. They wanted ultimate control.

****

Adama's first steps on Atlantean soil were not positive ones. As he got off the boat and waded to shore, he had a vision. Adama started to see red. He could see flames in his mind's eye. Adama could see women screaming and then he saw the eyes of an angel amidst the chaos; it was Rochelle.

As Adama walked along the shore, he knew Rochelle could see what he was seeing. She looked straight at him and placed her hand on her lips. 'Shhhhh', she said. 'Do not let the others know what you are seeing.'

How could Adama not let the elders know that war was coming? He was a high priest of Lemuria, he was there to save the people, not keep secrets from them!

However, Rochelle was from a high order of angels in heaven and was not to be disobeyed. Rochelle had served as an angel of Lemuria for thousands of years. She had acted as a second mother to him when Adama was a child. He would watch her in counsel with his parents and King Gaileth and Queen Aerlie. She had never given anything but helpful and truthful information, so Adama knew he had to trust her.

As they walked along the shore line, the head soldiers of Atlantis showed off their new boats, vessels and technology. The Lemurians admired the turbines the Atlanteans had made. The elders nodded at the new ships that had been built. The ships looked like monstrosities to Adama; they were larger and more powerful than Lemurian vessels. Adama was struck by the manpower they had working on the decks and was distressed by the way their workers were treated, as if they were menial staff. They toured the main lands while the Atlanteans lectured of their plans to strive for a new world, a better world. They nodded as they spoke with passion about rewards and recognition in return for hard-working troops. They spoke of promotions and ranking soldiers. They delighted in tales of hierarchy. These conversations made Adama shudder. Yes, the Atlanteans had grand ideas. Their forethought was precise and clever. However, they did not have the psychic ability of the Lemurians, nor the years of experience, nor the peace in their hearts.

The Atlanteans were an incredible race; they could clearly see the future. They had the capacity to see how the future of their turbines would create energy for the next five to ten years. Atlanteans spoke of how their psychic accuracy led them to believe their inventions would help change the next fifty years.

Adama had the ability to see thousands of years ahead, not fifty years ahead. This was the downfall of the Atlanteans. They could only see the more immediate future, not the long-term effects their current decisions would have on their entire race. This downfall was never going to be acknowledged by the minds of these simple natives.

Adama could see that in one hundred years' time, the constructions would fail. He could see the anger and resentment that the workers would have when their seniors did not ask them to go forward for promotions in rank or receive any advancement in their careers. He could see how workers would become negative as the turbines failed. Adama knew this would cause an outcry. Adama knew greed and envy would prevail in Atlantis. Adama could see that jealousy would reign throughout the Atlantean lands. Adama knew this was something that would never happen in Lemuria. Foresight was an important tool. Adama was a visionary, a skilled psychic; the Atlanteans did not seem to have this skill to the same extent. Adama saw their miscalculations and knew in his heart this had all been overlooked by the Atlanteans, as they were too busy reveling in their arrogance.

Adama's father's father always said that a great leader sees one thousand years ahead and works toward that. Adama's elders told him that with the power of psychic thought in Lemuria, this current day had been taken care of one thousand years ago. With forward thinking, Lemurian grandfathers had already prepared for war one thousand years before.

Atlantis was unaware of the Lemurian policies and philosophies. Adama continued to wander around Atlantis and nodded as the higher ranking Atlanteans showed off their land. Adama smiled through gritted teeth as he was told how their communities would greatly benefit from these inventions and how the Lemurians should think of doing the same.

The Atlanteans asked many questions and Rochelle told him to answer. Adama knew he was giving away clues to the motherland, but he always had to do as Rochelle said. Adama could see the other elders were just as nervous with the questioning, as they also had various psychic powers. However, they followed his lead. Rochelle professed that it was better to be truthful, otherwise the Lemurians would be considered to be as bad as the Atlanteans. The other elders in the group knew Adama had a plan.

Lemuria was made up of confusing circular grids and water. The Atlanteans now knew the best way into the main central grid in Lemuria. They knew where to dock their ships. They knew the Lemurian's boats were not as powerful as they thought. The Lemurian's boats were extremely powerful and they created their own energy supply to enhance the boat's speed. However, the Atlanteans did not seem impressed with their vessels.

As they left, the elders asked Adama many questions, and Adama saw Rochelle's face gesturing that he should not talk so he did not answer. Instead, Adama talked of the future of Lemuria in a positive way. Adama knew he was no longer in charge of his thoughts when Rochelle encouraged his mind to speak of good and peace. Adama knew Rochelle had to take over at this point, as Adama was sick to his stomach with fear.

****

After visiting Atlantis, Adama lay in bed night after night awaiting Rochelle's presence. He knew this angel would soon be telling him to take action, but she did not come. Adama could feel the people in Lemuria becoming angry with the Atlanteans and he could hear rumours of war. He knew there was to be an assembly of people secretly plotting war with

Atlantis. He knew and yet did nothing. He had to wait until Rochelle came to him.

Whenever Adama used psychic forethought to see the future he would see boats, mountains and thousands of Lemurians moving into a sacred space. It was as if he had to lead his people to a new land. Adama knew eventually they would be safe, but first they had to leave the motherland and get to this new country. He kept hold of this thought, hoping to manifest this beautiful image into reality.

He had the gift of manifestation. Adama believed that the more beautiful you could make images in your mind, the easier it would be to manifest the thought into reality. The priests, as a counsel, had to be very careful with this fact. They were not allowed to carelessly manifest. They were aware that they could conjure images in their heads and bring them to fruition.

Before the Atlanteans even existed, the elders and priests knew that people would start to use manifestation incorrectly: for personal gain, for greed, for jealous reasons. Therefore, the priests had to make a ruling: manifesting your wants with your mind was possible, but only if it was for the greater good. They knew there would be other species in existence that would try and manifest for personal gain or create wishes to harm others. This was forbidden to all in Lemuria, even the elders.

However, the images of a beautiful land under a mountain never left Adama's mind. Therefore, Adama knew that one day his manifestation would happen.

Adama also had the gift of clairvoyance, the gift of seeing guides. Adama knew Rochelle to be a powerful guide. However, he had other guides too: kings of the past, ancestors and other archangels that would come to counsel when they needed to make changes for the people.

Not long after the visit to Atlantis Adama slept very deeply one night, which was unusual. As he awoke in the morning, he felt an urgent need to look at the mountains outside his bedroom window. As he stared at the beauty of the mountain peaks, Adama saw the white wings of an angel looking at him. It was Rochelle. Adama bowed to her and knew it was time.

CHAPTER TEN

Adama's Story Continued

Rochelle said, 'He is ready.'

Adama rode to Damien immediately. The horses' hooves were muffled by the roars of frustration from the angered crowd as they rode through the villages. Then Adama saw him. Damien was standing on a barrel addressing many of the villagers. Adama remembered him immediately from when he was a child. Adama also clearly saw the angel guide Rochelle by his side.

Damien was talking to the masses. Adama noticed a clear sense of calm coming over them and knew this to be the work of Rochelle. Knowing Damien was the chosen warrior,

Adama had faith in his every word, his plea to those staring at him, his passion and his sense of duty. Adama tried to camouflage himself within the crowd until Rochelle encouraged him to step forward, but everyone was already looking at Adama with disdain.

As Damien's poetic voice carried over the crowds, Adama could see the people listening to him. It was as if Adama had lost control and Damien regained it. It was like watching the waning moon fall on Adama while the waxing moon shone on Damien. The apprentice had become the master. He had a skill to make people listen, a skill needed by the elders and the priesthood. The highest orders had done well to find this young man.

Adama walked off with Damien knowing Adama had much to teach the chosen one in a short space of time, while Rochelle was left behind.

CHAPTER ELEVEN

Adama the Teacher

With few words, Adama and Damien rushed to the temple library. Damien knew that he needed to follow and trust Adama. Adama could feel Damien's young energy and his inquisitive mind. They paced swiftly to the priests' temple. Damien was amazed by the almighty structures within the temple gates that he had previously only seen from afar.

Adama quickly assessed his psychic ability. He knew Damien had raw talent but he had not tapped into his spiritual path and this is where Adama came in. He was to teach Damien about his psychic skills. Teaching Damien quickly became his mission. Adama had no time to think, as he had to teach him swiftly about his amazing psychic ability and how to use these new found tools for the good of their people. If this young man could stop riots and bring peace, he had a place in leading the country and the masses in times of need.

They walked in the great doors of the temple where Adama introduced Damien to the elders. They bowed to him, knowing he was the chosen one. Damien was overwhelmed; he did not know where to look first, either at the magnificence of the building or at the room full of infamous elders. It felt like miracle upon miracle. They shook hands and then they were off to work.

CHAPTER TWELVE

Rochelle: The Psychic Angel

After a while, it was time for Rochelle to rejoin Damien and Adama. When firmly training Damien in the temple, Rochelle started to explain how he could use his sight to not only see but to also see the future more successfully. Damien was already involuntarily doing this. Rochelle explained how to switch the mind on to be able to see predictions on command.

Rochelle counseled, 'Close your eyes, Damien. Focus your mind on to your third eye in the middle of your forehead. See a purple haze in your third eye. This is your psychic eye. See it and open it. Relax your mind, Damien, and breathe slowly. Place both your feet firmly on the floor.'

Damien was learning quickly. He was calm. He was meditating much more easily than before. He was totally taken in by the angelic energy. Adama and Rochelle looked at each other, impressed with his will.

Adama stayed silent while observing, but interjected whenever Damien was losing focus. Damien became agitated that he wasn't learning quickly enough. What he did not understand was that he was learning faster and more accurately than anyone they'd ever seen.

Adama felt the importance of Damien's mission and prayed for him. Little did Damien know how important he would be to preserving Lemuria.

CHAPTER THIRTEEN

Zadiel's Story: The Community Priest:

As Zadiel walked through the great stone corridors toward the library, he could already hear the voices of Damien and Rochelle. They were speaking about the psychic third eye, how to be still and to trust one's premonitions. Zadiel knew immediately what was going on. It was clear the teachings with Damien, the chosen one, had begun.

Zadiel cried out, 'Adama! We need you urgently.'

Adama read Zadiel's thoughts and immediately left the room.

Zadiel's armour was heavy and his boots echoed down the corridor, but he still walked quickly as urgency prevailed. Adama dutifully followed.

Zadiel was the people's priest. It was his nature to care for everyone. He headed every community meeting. He cared so much for all people, animals and all living things in Lemuria.

Adama treated him equally, like a brother. They had different jobs to do, neither more significant than the other.

Zadiel spoke, 'Adama, listen. The priestess, Serene, has used her magic crystals to link in with Atlantis.'

The two priests stopped when they reached the great marble temple of the gods. The statues towered above them and the eyes of each god seemed to follow them around the room. The priests would often go there to pray and give thanks to the gods. Neither of them were keen on the talk of war in this sacred temple. The ceilings were so high that their voices travelled and echoed loudly. Adama looked up and saw statues of the great gods staring down at them. The scene was bittersweet for him.

Zadiel said, 'Serene is saying that the Atlanteans came here to learn the lands and now will attack again, but with more force. They will attack our sail boats and our larger vessels. They will attack us at sea if we try to go back to their land. The Atlanteans do not necessarily wish to kill us, but to teach us a lesson. Adama, you know more than any man that the Atlanteans do not have the power of forethought like we do. Adama, they do not see this will only anger the gods!'

Zadiel looked up to the high marble columns and with his hands in prayer position gave respect to the gods' temple.

Zadiel continued, 'Atlantis does not see that this will destroy the future of all lands, not just ours, but theirs too, if they continue to try to rule us. Adama, what should we do? We must fight back! I know we should not, but that's the only thing we can do now. You must come and talk to Serene.'

Adama nodded in agreement. Zadiel led him to the priestesses' chambers.

CHAPTER FOURTEEN

Serene's Story: An Unveiling

A beautiful, mysterious being stood in the middle of the priestesses' chambers. As the priests walked through to the ladies' quarters a sense of calm came over them. They took one look at Serene and saw a quiet and calm beauty: serene by nature and by name. This stunning Lemurian was like no other. With her long dark hair, dark skin and dark eyes she stood out in Lemuria among the many blonde haired, blue-eyed women. Serene stood in the middle of the room while the elders watched. The priests formed a semicircle around her and knew not to interrupt.

Serene spoke infrequently. She looked as if she were in a trance as she flittered through different conversations. It was as if she were touring the lands of Atlantis and then relaying what she was seeing back to the priests. Serene had always been incredibly psychic and a natural healer.

Although all Lemurians were healers, Serene had a deeper skill. Serene saw illness as colour and could lift the colour and illness out of people to cure them. All Lemurians knew that everything was made of energy. If everything was made of energy, that meant they are also made of energy. Energy was constantly moving and changing shape. Serene could move and shift the 'bad' or sick energy. She could also turn this into a healthy energy; she was gifted in deep healing. Serene worked with another priestess named Amara to create symbols for this healing technique. Amara was the priestess of the sea and the two of them would teach others to learn these symbols and become healers. The two priestesses had an ultimate vision: they hoped all Lemurians would soon be using this intense healing ability to lift the frequency of the planet. Healing was not to be kept secret but was to be shared. Serene wanted to help teach women and children how to self-heal.

The priestesses believe the body should be honoured. If all were to honour their bodies, all would be able to self-heal.

Serene's chamber was full of light with beautiful, mountainous views. She held a pink object in her hands. The priests and the elders all waited for her to speak again.

Serene held out the object, a crystal skull, and said, 'Show me'.

Serene began, 'My head hurts. I can hear the cries of the people. They must do all they can to stop this disaster … tidal waves … people screaming. I can hear the cries.'

Serene's disjointed sentences were all they needed to understand that a catastrophe was heading their way.

Serene fell to the floor sobbing. She appeared to be living what she saw. She had a way of feeling what other people felt. In psychic terms, this is called being a clairsentient.

When Serene saw something, she also felt it. It was heartbreaking to watch as Serene suffered the fate of others. She felt it was her duty to help others, so she wanted to feel every inch of their pain.

Serene continued, 'The waves are getting higher. People are fleeing. They don't know whether to go uphill or down to the seas. I can see hundreds of people running. They are taking their babies and their belongings and many are heading for the boats. The vessels are full of people. They do not know where they are fleeing to. However, they know they need to leave. Where are they all going?'

She looked up, confused. She stopped looking at the crystal skull. 'What am I seeing?' she asked.

Adama stepped forward.

Adama answered, 'The gods will give us the information at the right time, Serene. They always do. Just keep showing me your vision. You know the psychic rules, Serene. Priestesses have all been given a gift. Use it in the right way. You are being shown what we need to know from the gods right now. We are not to question what is being shown. We are to accept it and know this will aide us.'

Serene bowed to Adama and carried on. She lifted the crystal and stared at it intently.

Serene commanded, 'Show me!' She seemed to demand her insight to work for her on command. This seemed unusual yet astonishing that this psychic could talk to her own ability. Serene got up and moved around the spherical stone room, looking at nobody in particular. She was staring hard as if she were trying to see something the rest of them could not see.

Serene described her vision, 'I can hear water...huge waves ...water that will cover Lemuria! The vision is turning. Now I can see a hill. This is unnerving. I cannot see the ocean but I can hear water, lots of it. I can see the land trembling, like the water is coming from below. I can see the people looking up the hill. They look with fear in their eyes. They look at each other as they run. They are looking for answers but there aren't any. People run and scream as they look over their shoulders at the gushing water that is unstoppable. I see a wave and I hear a tremble as the land shakes. I do not understand this but I can tell you I can see our land shaking - Lemuria shaking. I see a huge wave. One that is bigger than any wave I have ever encountered. The wave will come. Lemuria will sink.'

She sobbed again.

Serene cried, 'I must be wrong. This cannot be true.'

Adama replied, 'You know you are not wrong, Serene. Your gift of insight is too good. You have never been wrong. Plus, you are purely channeling the knowledge of the crystal in your hand.'

Serene asked, 'How can this happen to us? Why is this going to happen?' She cried uncontrollably on the cold marble floor. Elders rushed to her aide.

Serene protested, 'This has nothing to do with Atlantis or being at war. This is a natural disaster. This is not fair. We have worked so hard for this land and for each other. We have taught people how to love, how to be self-sufficient and how to make a life compared to heaven on earth. This is no reward.'

Adama spoke again, 'The Atlanteans have struck once and it looks like they will strike again. This will anger the gods and the gods may choose to sink us all. Whatever happens is right to happen. We must follow their wishes. We cannot fight against the fate of Lemuria. However, we must stick together and do all we can to not anger the gods. We must remain peaceful and loving. This is the Lemurian way - the only way.'

Serene asked, 'Why were we not shown the exact timing of the Atlanteans last invasion? I could have stopped the war! I could have helped save innocent people!' Serene's empathy for all was clear to see.

Adama responded, 'The gods know best Serene; they tell us only what we need not what we want'.
Serene was sobbing uncontrollably. The visions were so real to her. Serene loved the motherland as much as the next Lemurian and

to see it sink was a terrifying sight. Sometimes Serene wished she could not see these images, especially the vision of the fall of Lemuria.

CHAPTER FIFTEEN

Serene's Life

Serene came from a family of intellectuals. Her mother, Xenia, was also a spiritual healer and Serene learned her craft at a very young age. Her mother had a soft, gentle energy that clearly saw sickness and healing. Xenia used the crystals from the earth - the Lemurian seed crystals, to help heal people. Her mother would add her healing to the power of the crystal and give it to people who needed the healing. Xenia was kind and true and dedicated to the people.

Serene saw her mother's dedication from an early age and began to follow her good deeds and heal others.

Xenia humoured Serene at first and let this young child follow her to the healing chambers, which were crystalline caves. After watching Serene's natural ability and genteel approach with patients, Xenia realised Serene's gift and potential. Xenia could clearly see the mighty angel Rochelle standing behind Serene when she was performing healing. Xenia was flabbergasted by this. Rochelle had only appeared to her a few times in her life, yet Rochelle seemed to be with Serene all the time helping with her healing. Serene was clearly a natural Lemurian healer. But now, Serene would be known as an angelic Lemurian healer; she had a rare gift indeed. Xenia knew that Serene was meant for greatness.

Serene knew she had energy around her, but sometimes she was not exactly certain who or what it was. Serene felt the angels around her, but she sometimes could not distinguish between them. Serene could not see Rochelle, but eventually learnt the energy of her. Serene's gift was a unique one, as she was a natural healer, clairsentient and clairvoyant too. Her clairsentient ability meant she could feel the emotions of others. Serene sensed people's personalities easily. This natural healer could tell how someone was going to react. She had feelings about what was going to happen.

Serene was also demonstrably clairvoyant, meaning she could see things that were about to happen. Serene's psychic visions seemed to work even better when she held crystals. Crystals held and absorbed natural energy and Serene could sense that energy. With the help of Rochelle, Serene could hold any Lemurian seed crystal, focus her psychic eye on the crystal and receive futuristic images in her mind. Serene would then dictate these images to the elders.

CHAPTER SIXTEEN

Rochelle's Story: Patience

Damien exclaimed, 'I just can't do it. It doesn't work like that. I cannot just see things on request!'

Rochelle replied, 'Yes you can, you just switch it on. Tell me what you see.' Rochelle had endless patience. She stood behind Damien urging him to continue. They didn't have much time.

Damien paced toward the window, staring at the mountain, wishing to be a warrior again, wishing he could go outside and be with his friends.

Damien said, 'I can't, it won't work. It happens only when it wants to.'

Rochelle urged Damien, 'Just try.'

Damien became very quiet and sat on the floor. He had a habit of sitting on the ground when he was trying to switch on his psychic ability. Damien didn't know why he did this, but the angel knew that he was obtaining energy from the land itself. He was charging himself with Earth energy and grounding himself. A great way to switch on his psychic ability was to put both feet on the ground to charge himself up.

Damien spoke, 'OK. I can hear that wave again. It's the same scene, Rochelle. The wave comes and everyone runs down the hill to the boats. I know you want details, Rochelle. But I see the same thing. I'll do the breathing technique you taught me to go deeper.'

Damien put both hands in his lap and closed his eyes. He sat still on the floor.

Damien cried out, 'I see Adama! He is on a horse heading for the boats. People are marching behind him slowly, but some people are staying. They are sitting on the floor. They are singing. Some are praying and some are holding hands. They are sitting in ever decreasing circles. They are all connected. It's as if they are sitting in a sequence. It looks like a maze. They seem happy to sit even though there is chaos around them. I cannot be seeing this right. Why would everyone be sitting down peacefully when there is chaos around them? It is as if they don't see the waves.'

Damien turned to see Adama standing in the hallway.

Adama addressed Damien, 'Come now, Damien. You have learned well, but now you must see Zadiel.'

Being the head priest of all communities, Zadiel commanded respect. Zadiel had a warrior's physique with a strong outline. He was one of the tallest Lemurians, so tall that people would stand back in amazement when he walked through the streets. He had a large presence and looked like he was made of steel. The common people were tentative about Zadiel due to his huge stature. However, his loved ones knew that you could not meet a kinder person. Zadiel cared not for himself but for the welfare of the people. His spiritual gift was the gift of love. Zadiel openly poured pure love from his heart to the people, the land and the animals of Lemuria and would die for the them all.

He cared in equal measure for his immediate family and the people of the motherland. Zadiel was a high priest who took care of all the other high priests and priestesses. Zadiel worked with ascended masters and the gods for the good of Lemuria.

Zadiel was aware of the darker energies that had created Atlantis and he knew how this would affect the future of Lemuria. The Lemurians were a highly spiritual race that were created to live in harmony. However, where there was light, there was also dark. Zadiel was warned by the gods that there was a co-race that was being created that would ultimately form Atlantis.

Zadiel's task had been given to him by the gods: Zadiel was not to war with Atlantis. He was to keep all of Lemuria safe. The safety of the land, the trees, the plants, the animals, the energy, the Lemurian people was all within his care.

Zadiel worried about how to maintain peace and how to handle the chaos that would soon come. He knew that future species would need the land unscathed and therefore did not want anything harmed. Zadiel did not want to anger the gods so he knew he had to obey. He was shown in his dreams that future races would find Lemuria.

The high priest had the gift of forethought so he could see millions of years ahead. He knew he needed to protect Mother Earth as future races would not. He knew that even though Atlantis would try and destroy his home, the

Lemurians home, he had to think further than himself and his race. Zadiel was ultimately given the hardest task of all Lemurians.

Zadiel was born into a family of greatness and he was born with a heart big enough for all. He always loved more than he needed to. Zadiel was always forward thinking. As a child he would never go out and play with the other children. He would rather listen to his father and his father's friends talk of their common goal to create a harmonised society, a peaceful community and the enhancements they would make to the motherland. Lemuria was his passion from a young age.

His concern for the welfare of the entire community meant Zadiel could not switch off from his task. The mere thought of Atlantis gaining power gave him a constant excruciating pain in his heart. Zadiel was continually thinking about his next move to save the people.

Damien and Adama quickly arrived at the high court where Zadiel's shadow dominated the grandeur of the enormous, historical room.

Zadiel spoke, 'We will secure the land and take the people away. We cannot let innocent people suffer. We must take them in boats to other lands. We must ask the gods where to take them. I will pray to the gods for answers.'

Zadiel was in the high court, standing in the circle of the greats, pleading with the counsel. Because he had a great connection with the gods, Zadiel knew the counsel would listen to him. He could connect and hear the gods better than anyone else on the land of Mu and they knew it.

After a long, heartfelt speech, Zadiel stormed out of the counsel and looked up to the skies. 'What are we to do?', he asked.

Zadiel always felt the answers arising within him from the ground, the sacred earth. A female voice started talking inside his head. This was the voice of one of the gods.

The god said, 'Zadiel, you must take them away, the ones who want to go. Leave this land to us. We know what is best. You have done everything you can to protect the land, but now you must protect your people.'

Zadiel responded, 'Where shall I take them?' He was angry that he was to leave his beloved land.

The god replied, 'We will tell you when it is time to go. You are not to gather the troops just yet, as no one is to be fearful. On our command and with love, you will take them to a new land.'

Zadiel could not believe what he was hearing. His thoughts were like flickers of angry flames.

Zadiel protested, 'A new land? Not Lemuria? Where is this land? We have been safe here! What if we do not find the land? What if some people will not come with me? Am I to leave them behind to be enveloped by the waves of the sea?'

'Zadiel, I need you!' It was Adama.

Standing outdoors by the old wise oak trees, Damien was introduced formally to a stunned and rather silent Zadiel.

It was here that Zadiel witnessed Damien's psychic insight more intently. Zadiel had already been shown the chosen one in his dreams; he was just as impressive in the flesh. Damien, Adama, Rochelle and Zadiel sat chatting under the oaks about skill, gifts, psychic powers and fighting. They made a dynamic team, connecting to the gods, angels and clairvoyance. With these skills, they knew they could conquer. Although none of them knew exactly what was going to happen next.

CHAPTER SEVENTEEN

Amara's Story: The Priestesses Chambers

Serene was on the floor. Amara, the great goddess of the sea and the natural healer, walked in to Serene's chambers where she saw the elders scattered around, helpless.

Amara asked, 'What is wrong, Serene?'

Serene was sobbing and could not answer.

Amara put her hand out in front of her and stared at it. It was not clear what she was doing. She tilted her head to one side and looked on inquisitively.

Amara exclaimed, 'Oh no!'

Amara had put her hand into Serene's visions. Amara had seen the waves that would ultimately cause the fall of Lemuria.

Amara's hands were powerful. She had the gift of seeing the future with her hands. Her hands created a channel of healing for the land, the sea and the people of Lemuria.

She was an almighty healer. Known as the priestess of the ocean, Amara was a great attribute to Lemuria. Amara was a right-hand priestess to Adama, the leading priest of Lemuria.

Amara would often be called to counsel to use her hands to show the future. She could use her body to feel the future. If the future did not look bright in Lemuria, her body was sure to tell her: she would become sick, anxious and distraught with headaches the day before something awful was about to happen to her beloved land.

Amara was a powerful priestess whose energy was felt by anyone who thought about her. Amara had an ancient energy, she was one of the oldest souls. By saying her name, the people of Lemuria could feel her presence in the healing of the land and oceans surrounding Lemuria.

Amara could command the energy of Lemuria to work with her. If she wanted to see the future of Lemuria she could command it by using the energy of the sea. She was often found standing at the edge of the ocean, charging her energy by the sea.

As Amara stared into the ocean, she could see moving pictures of the future of Lemuria. It was as if she had plugged herself in to the wisdom of the ocean.

Amara helped Serene to her feet.

Amara spoke, 'We must do what we have to do. Yes, the land is changing. Yes, there will be disruption, but the opinion of the gods is that things must change. Many Lemurians will soon be receiving the same images of the future, but it is all about how we interpret these images. It is easy to be fatalistic and say it is the end of our time, but we can ask the gods why this is happening and create something better for our people. If our land is to change and we are to be here no more, then we must accept our future. The waves will come. Adama will have counsel with the gods. The angels will walk this earth again. We will be made aware of the waves and some will take the boats. Some will be instructed to leave. Some will remain, as they love their land too much and they will drown with the land.'

Amara had a way of explaining things from a higher perspective. She understood the precision needed when using psychic ability. Amara knew that to see a vision of the future was one thing, but to interpret it was another. It is well known that those who have a psychic gift need to be very careful when being descriptive with their premonitions. Emotions, advice and visions needed to be given exactly as they were seen and not misinterpreted or attached to people's own opinion. Amara knew the importance of knowing where the information was coming from. Is this coming from ego? A place of fear? Is this coming from imagination? A negative energy source? Or is this a real premonition?

Amara was an old wise soul whose guides were the gods, the seas and Mother Earth. Therefore, her source of information was completely viable.

Amara said, 'I call the gods. I call you in to this counsel. I muster all my strength to hear and see you as I praise you.'

Serene walked forward in prayer, adding to Amara's powerful energy.

The moment the two of them started to pray, energy filled the room. It felt electric. Amara's eyes were now wide open and she seemed to be channeling the gods.

Amara started to speak in a more mechanic tone, 'We will tell you in due course. However, there will be floods. Warring with Atlantis was not our intention. It is time for a new race to start. It is time for Lemurians to come home. Lemurians are not supposed to feel anger and resentment, this is not the way. The world is changing, now learn to accept it.'

CHAPTER EIGHTEEN

Damien's Story: Inner Turmoil

Damien was walking around the temple grounds alone. To be allowed into the great temples was such an honour, and yet all Damien could feel was resentment. He stood on the balcony overlooking the waterfalls on the east side of the mountain and sighed. If only his friends could enter these temples and see the beauty. If only he could feel happy as he stared at the breathtaking views. Damien could not fully enjoy the magnitude of the landscape. He felt lost amongst the giant pillars of the great halls.

Damien felt very much alone. He was worried he would lose his friends because of his new life, his new obligations and his new psychic gifts.

Although all Lemurians were positive and spiritual, Damien had increased his spiritual capabilities and knew this would bring huge changes to his life; changes in him and changes to his circle of friends and networks.

Was he ready to change his life just because his spiritual self had shifted?

He felt he did not have a choice in this and that his spiritual self was now ruling his body. He felt he had a duty to follow his angel guide Rochelle and also his intuition.

'Charles!' Damien called from the upper balconies. Charlie was unmissable even from a distance due to his unique, dark looks and beautiful gelding horse, Sirius.

Damien and Charlie were childhood friends. Damien had fond memories of playing and sword fighting with Charlie, mainly because Damien always won.

Damien never understood how he was able to beat his friend all the time, but he always knew which way Charlie would strike. Damien was now starting to believe it was his psychic ability that helped him as a child. He was beginning to realise that the calmer he was when predicting future events, the more his psychic ability flowed.

Charlie looked up and saw Damien from afar. Damien started to run and got to the iron gates of the temples that looked onto the market area.

'Have you heard the rumours?' Charlie inquired from the other side of the gates. The two were the best of friends yet now iron gates separated them.

Charlie continued, 'Something about the Atlanteans coming back and a wave engulfing the land?'

Damien replied, 'Don't believe all you hear Charlie.'

Charlie flicked his dark hair back as he dismounted his horse. Charlie took great care in his appearance; his yellow cloak was in perfect order as he stood as close to Damien as he could get.

Charlie responded, 'I would never leave this land! This is my home, where my family is. I will stay if there is trouble. I will defend my land. Some are talking about fleeing across the ocean. Many are talking about taking the boats. I am not going. I am not sure why there is even a fuss. Plus, what would we do then? Be stuck out at sea? I am angry the gods haven't told us what to do now.'

Charlie was a passionate young man, a fighter through and through. His passion outweighed his common sense and always would. He spoke so loudly that the market traders looked agitated. The slight murmur of war among the people was enough for arguing to commence. Charlie did not care who heard him. He was ready to fight for his land.

Charlie asked, 'Where have you been Damien? And why on earth are you in the temple grounds?'

Damien replied, 'I just had to deliver a message, that's all.' Damien lied hoping Charlie would not pick up on it.

'I'll see you soon Charlie'. Damien looked down to his feet as he spoke, avoiding eye contact.

Damien could smell the anger from Charlie and could feel the frustration from his aura. Damien knew he did not fit in his group of friends anymore. Change had already begun.

CHAPTER NINETEEN

Aurelia's Story: The Unsung Hero

A simple girl of Lemuria stood watching half her people leave for battle. Aurelia had been a quiet bystander since the very start. She had kept a watchful eye over warriors while they trained and bragged about winning wars.

Aurelia looked like an ordinary Lemurian. Standing at six feet, she was a similar height to most of the girls her age. Her blonde hair fell past her waist and was tied with flowers similar to other Lemurian town girls.

Aurelia's common-place looks were a huge contrast to her complex and unique personality.

She had no husband who would fight, nor a father to shed a tearful goodbye for. Aurelia did have her younger brother, Bodean, who was too young to fight. Aurelia spent her time pondering that one day her younger sibling would become a mindless warrior like the others.

Aurelia may not have been a priestess nor did she have royal blood in her veins, but her unprecedented talents as a sorceress would have amazed the elders and perhaps even the gods.

Preferring to spend her time in nature, Aurelia practiced her craft quietly in the forest. Aurelia did not like the congested towns.

She was a multifaceted being: plain clothed and unnoticeable on the outside, yet possessing an overworked, busy mind and a sultry expression on her face. Aurelia was an enigma to the few that got close to her.

Aurelia's distress came from her ability to see future wars. As a sorceress, she knew the warriors would eventually fall to their death. Aurelia had sensed the naivety and ignorance of the warriors as the troops had marched to the ships seeking revenge a few days before.

Aurelia was claircognizant, thus she had the power of knowing the future. Aurelia was overly aware that having the power of 'knowing' without the power of 'speaking up', was no power at all.

Aurelia's heavy heart caused negative thought patterns in her busy mind: 'The elders will not speak with a common town girl like me regardless of my powers. I cannot keep letting these people sail to their deaths! But what if my knowing is incorrect? I will look such a fool!'

Aurelia felt that being claircognizant was a curse. Preferring solitude, Aurelia did not mix with other people to share her tale of woe. She was aware that the Lemurian's reign on the motherland was coming to an end. Aurelia would carry this knowledge like a heavy burden until the end of her short days.

Aurelia was not educated in sorcery, she had not been schooled in the art of psychic ability and she lacked knowledge of the healing modalities; she just knew all of this from birth. She could extract healing properties from any plant by mixing flowers and herbs from the forest.

Aurelia would practice on her brother when he grazed his knee or got sick. Aurelia instinctively knew precisely which plants to go to for the right medicine. She started to practice mixing herbs and plants with crystals. Aurelia's well-kept secret resided in the labyrinth of the forests. This is where Aurelia discovered the hidden crystal caves.

Aurelia discovered crystals embedded in rocks and in the earth that were hidden from the untrained eye. She spent many days in the caves, staring in wonder. She knew the crystals to be rose quartz and Lemurian seed crystals. Aurelia could effortlessly feel the healing from the crystals as she sat in the stillness of the caves.

Aurelia knew it was not her place to remove these crystals. However, she wanted to use them for their healing abilities. Whenever her brother was sick, she would carry him to the caves, never revealing their exact location to others.

It was a sad time for Aurelia as she had spent the last few days standing helplessly watching her people march to their eventual death. Aurelia was devastated that she would not be able to take the wounded to the secret healing caves as no one was going to listen to a common town girl.

Aurelia had the gift of premonition. Without trying, this wise soul could see things way beyond the here and now. Aurelia saw events in the future as if she were watching a film. Looking toward her left hand side, she was shown a movie scene of what the future held. Aurelia stared at this movie, knowing it was accurate. She was shown scenes with such detail that it felt undoubtedly genuine. Aurelia passed the hours staring at these visions, knowing the significance of these premonitions.

For the tender age of eighteen, Aurelia was extremely wise. Aurelia's quiet, youthful demeanor masked the knowledge she kept to herself. Aurelia hid many secrets within.

CHAPTER TWENTY

Aurelia's Story Continued

Aurelia had been watching the priests and priestesses from the forest for some time. She had a tendency to follow people without being noticed. The sorceress would hide behind the magnificent trees in the woodlands behind the counsel chambers. Aurelia watched the priests and priestesses hurry to the gods' temple for their urgent counsel meetings.

Aurelia would spy on the elder's holding counsel. Aurelia cleverly learned that each person's voice had its own unique vibration. Aurelia learned the energy of each voice vibration and tuned in to them. She was often found standing quietly by a wise, old, oak tree that acted like a whispering wall. The priests' voices would travel from the temple to the old oak while Aurelia used the tree to clearly hear what they said. Aurelia knew they were thinking of leaving Lemuria and wanted to help. Nevertheless, she also knew of her status in Lemuria. Who would listen to her? She felt she was of no importance. Still, Aurelia could not help but feel it was her duty to help heal in the caves.

Aurelia wondered whether she should tell people about the crystal caves and if it would enhance her chances of becoming a healer that people would recognise and respect. She was sick of being the girl with no name.

Even though all people were seen as equals regardless of rank or skill set, Aurelia couldn't help feeling like she was a nobody. Aurelia pondered to herself: 'If I achieved my full potential as a spiritual healer, maybe I would belong.'

Although Aurelia was content being at her brother's side completing menial tasks, she knew that she was destined for more. She knew she was fated to do something spectacular with her life even though her family title never lent itself to this idea of greatness.

Aurelia's mind was forever busy, full of the words she would say to the elders. Aurelia had numerous descriptive words explaining her position, but was lacking in the confidence to speak them. Or was she?

CHAPTER TWENTY-ONE

Roberto's Story: King Of The Seas

Roberto was fondly known as King of the Seas. He was a naval officer of Lemuria. He understood the seas, the weather and the earth well; he was known as a human compass.

Roberto's unusual psychic gift of reading the elements left others in wonder. He seemed to understand fire, wind, water and the earth better than any man. Roberto was known as an unsung hero who did not like the limelight. He was strong and tough, yet not an attention seeker. He was a gentle action man. Roberto did not need recognition or a round of applause for being psychically gifted. He felt his gift came naturally to him, so why the need for praise?

Roberto had a good reputation in the navel unit for accurately knowing the seas. He was commended for his courage and disciplined nature. There was a different side to Roberto, however. He was also sensitive and loving. He held the love of his wife and his beautiful child close to his heart. Roberto had been known to weep while away from his family at sea. His love for his wife and child had spanned one hundred and sixty-five years. He was one hundred and eighty-five years old but still looked twenty-five and was very handsome. His rugged good looks and gentle, soft eyes often had the ladies swooning. Yet Roberto only had eyes for his family.

His wife, Cleopatra, was a natural beauty. She had very long blonde hair and pointed elf-like features. Cleopatra's eyes were mesmerizing; they were so blue they looked almost indigo in colour, like the ocean. Roberto had been in love with her since he was a little boy; they grew up together. Without her, his world would end. She gave him the courage to go out to sea where he faced wars, heavy storms, battled Mother Earth's natural disasters. Cleopatra gave him all the courage he needed. Roberto's bravery was greater than any other naval officer anyone had ever seen. Although Roberto was not the captain of the ship nor was he of any ranking due to his heritage and his desire to stand in the shadows, he was a well-respected Lemurian.

Lemurians were a race that originally evolved without ego. Lemurians all believed in nature, respect for the earth and love for other human beings. They initially paid homage to their elders, the priests and priestesses. At the same time, they also believed everyone to be equal. Although times were changing in the motherland, as admiration for the elders was on the decline, Roberto was still the epitome of a true Lemurian.

Roberto had been instructed to get the Criterion ready, the ship he often sailed. He worked on this particular twenty-five-ton vessel for numerous years and had helped to create it. The ship held the crew, food, drink, building materials and even farm animals. It had a mast taller than anything he had ever created before.

The vessel amazed Roberto on a daily basis. He knew every inch of it by heart, even the cracks in the woodwork on the floor where other shipmates had been careless. The disciplined sailor took his job very seriously. He could often be found smoothing the sides of the ship or cleaning the floors even though it was not his job to do so.

The captain of the ship informed him he must get ready to sail. Roberto did not need to know why. He did not care for war nor the recent problems and threats he witnessed from Atlanteans. Roberto did as he was told because he was a master to the sea.

Roberto's gift was a very interesting one. Roberto could command fire to spark, just by thinking about it. Roberto was a master of the flame. He enjoyed working with fire. He understood that flames were used for meditative purposes. Flames enhanced his energy and lifted his vibration so he could become more psychic. Fire energized him similarly to the way food energized others. Roberto was fascinated by the magic of fire.

Roberto could also easily sense Mother Earth. He was clairsentient when it came to the earth: he could sense her. Nicknamed the King of the Seas, Roberto understood Mother Earth's need to be respected and looked after.

Roberto's ability to grow crops on the motherland was phenomenal. He intuitively understood which soil to use for growing vegetables so his harvests were always the most sumptuous. Others were often astounded by the vegetables he could grow. Even when no one had grown any crops due to bad soil and fermentation, Roberto's grew perfectly. He explained that he manifested the crops by conversing with Mother Earth before he grew them. Roberto also spoke to her to ascertain when to water crops and when to leave them to seed. Other Lemurians would look on in wonder as they had to manifest their food in a different way due to bad harvest.

This is why Roberto was the master of the seas. He understood fire and how much of it was needed to power each vessel. He could understand Mother Earth and responded to her requests by steering the ship intuitively, even if his fellow sailors felt he was steering straight into a storm.

Roberto could also sense the ocean. He understood what great waves were to be avoided and knew where the sun shone too brightly or not enough. Roberto mainly understood how to get the energy from the sea, using Mother Earth as his guide. Without him, the naval crew would not be anywhere near as successful.

Roberto had recently been whispering to Mother Earth, as he knew she was not happy with the upset between the Lemurians and the people of Atlantis. Mother Earth felt the talk of war and sensed greed within the evolving races.

Roberto had lived for almost two hundred years on the earth, previously in a harmonious time. However, he started to notice more angst from the Lemurians recently. Conversations created negative energies around groups of sailors. He heard tales of hate toward the people of Atlantis. Talks used to be of love, family and creation, never war and hate!

Roberto respected Mother Earth, he knew his people merely lived on her planet as guests. If she became angry with them, they would know it. Mother Earth could easily create great winds, all-encompassing fires and eruptions they could not imagine. Lemurians would not be able to respond to Mother Earth's fury.

Roberto was a simple man with fundamental needs. He held his knowledge of Mother Earth close to his broad chest. Roberto was intuitive enough to know he would not be fully understood if he explained the wrath of Mother Earth. Plus, Roberto had no desire for ongoing negative discussions about his beloved land. So, he went about his business with quiet confidence.

Roberto followed his orders: they would sail toward Atlantis at sunrise.

CHAPTER TWENTY-TWO

Jonas and the Sailors from Atlantis

Jonas, a sailor from Atlantis, had been sailing for three days on a very small ship with a small crew. The long boat was a thin, wooden vessel with ornate carvings on the front. Jonas was known as a middle rower. Jonas did not take this role seriously. He had a few friends on board and they would all laugh and make jokes to make the time pass with ease. The sailors didn't particularly like being on the boat. It was a tough job, especially when the sun was beating down on them.

They had been sailing for three moons. The deck was stained with sweat and ocean spray. The vessel's stench was a mixture of working men and fish. Jonas felt the sun on his back like a fireball. Jonas ignored the battle of the elements.

Jonas was quite a young soul at twenty-four. He was very strong, handsome and popular with the women of Atlantis, yet too young of heart for true love. Jonas would have rather spent time play fighting with his friends. He was happy being on his own. He had a strong heart and when he wanted to settle, he would.

His uniqueness made him stand out in Atlantis. He was much shorter than an average Atlantean. At just six feet tall, others towered above him. However, he was still popular with the females of Atlantis due to his charm, very dark eyes, darker skin, good looks and his strength. His arms were very muscular, he was broad chested and very handy with a sword. Jonas' face was so beautiful that people often stopped and stared at him. He kept his hair long and unkempt and he had a carefree attitude, all adding to the attraction.

This one of a kind sailor would much rather have spent time with his dog and his sister's children than spend time trying to woo a lady. He felt this was pointless.

As Jonas rowed, he overheard the captain talking about Lemuria and was aware they were going to war with the people of Mu.

Jonas stared up at the sun and saw seagulls. Land was close. He had been praying for rest for hours now.

Jonas was looking forward to seeing his homeland again. He was proud of his land and wanted to protect Atlantis. Jonas was aware that not all was well in Atlantis. Quite often he heard the elders of Atlantis arguing, becoming angry as they talked about the oceans, other lands and how Atlantis wanted to conquer other unknown continents.

In Atlantis, Jonas knew he was a rower and was firmly aware of his basic life: he was never going to be an elder or have any status or recognition.

Jonas had recently noticed aggravation on land. Being at sea for months on end gave Jonas time to reflect about his homeland. He was quick to notice differences in his people. Jonas had been made aware of competition amongst his friends, comparing houses and ownership titles, crops and who had the best animals. Jonas was intuitive enough to know that change was ripe in Atlantis, he was also aware this transformation was not for the better.

Jonas was excessively strong but he also had the gift of agility. He was very well known within his community for having play fights with his friends and always winning, not because he was the tallest or the strongest, but because his quick thinking and sharp movements baffled his attacker. He could jump very high and do backflips, tumbles and other moves that confused his opponent. Jonas' ability was the talk of the homeland. He did not take this gift seriously and only used it for play fighting. However, he prayed that one day he would be in the main arenas jumping over bulls with his unusual gift. Jonas continued daydreaming about bull jumping in Atlantis while he rowed monotonously.

****

Yonassis stood tall and argued to no avail. Yonassis was head of the Atlantean crew of the long boat heading to Lemuria. He knew he had to answer to the captain though. Yonassis had heard a lot about the Lemurians and felt that his they would welcome communication rather than to go to war. Yonassis thought that the Lemurians would rather talk with gentle ease than fight. He wanted to use this approach, however the captain, Georgus, wanted to show that Atlantis meant business. Georgus wanted to go to war if the people of Mu would not stop telling them how to run their lands. The argument between the two continued.

Yonassis was surrounded by the energy of the elders. His father and forefathers who were no longer on the land were still around him in a spiritual sense. He had the gift of mediumship and could see those who had passed over. The forefathers could choose to leave the land, but they preferred be part of the earth; their souls remained with Yonassis. Some decided to die and had been buried so that one day others would be able to find their remains and gain insight about this time in history. Even though their bodies were in the ground, their essence remained with Yonassis.

Yonassis would often show his annoyance to Georgus, the captain. Yonassis would tell him that his forefathers had given him insights about what was going to happen if they started warring without compassion. However, Georgus was too strong in his own policies: he longed for blood.

As Jonas carried on rowing, Yonassis talked openly to anyone who would listen about the spirits that surrounded him. Captain Georgus could not see the spirits of Yonassis' forefathers, so Georgus chose not to listen. Georgus himself was not gifted with psychic ability. The captain struggled to understand predictions until they happened. This gave Georgus no reason to believe that going to war again was wrong.

Yonassis had a very gentle, sensitive and spiritual way about him. He would often be found meditating and talking to his forefathers to ask of their opinion about the trouble between Atlantis and Lemuria. Yonassis was repeatedly informed that there would be a great war and that this conflict would be very destructive if they did not come to terms with each other. If they continued with brutality, all would be lost. Yonassis looked to the sea, forlorn.

Captain Georgus had great presence and was sturdily built. Georgus stood much taller and wider than anyone else on board the Atlantean long boat. Georgus wanted a war and Yonassis did not, but Georgus was ultimately in charge of the vessel and all those on board.

Captain Georgus was openly grateful that the gods let Atlanteans live on their beautiful land. Attending slaughters for the gods or leaving gifts for the gods was his favourite pastime. Treasure, jewels and gold would be left by the mighty captain. He believed Atlantean lands were immensely spiritual. Georgus believed the weather to be a warning from the gods and thought that if there were storms, it only meant that the gods were displeased.

Georgus' strong beliefs were both his strengths and weaknesses. He did not have time for family or to be in love because he was too busy loving and protecting his land. He was so protective and territorial over Atlantis that he was not going to let the Lemurians tell him what to do. "Who were the Lemurians to dictate to me!" He thought.

The captain did not want to know what the Lemurians thought just because they had been around longer. To Georgus, this did not make the Lemurians the wiser race, it just made them arrogant.

Atlantis had a new energy, it was fresh and modern. Atlanteans were excited about their own new ideas, new boats, new systems; they were proud of their land and it was worth fighting for.

Georgus was not listening to Yonassis anymore. He was the captain of the boat; he knew his power and would not back down. He could not wait to meet the priests of Lemuria; he would strike them if he had to. Georgus would show his warrior skills immediately and stress that the Lemurians should not have concerned themselves with Atlantis. Georgus would give them a warning they would not forget that the Lemurians needed to stay far away.

Georgus would often be heard speaking of the unknown continents. Yes, there were other continents as well as Atlantis and Lemuria. Atlantis was aware of this and Georgus thought that if they wanted to govern them all, that was their businesses and not for Lemuria to interfere with.

****

Jonas carried on rowing and knew that if his two superiors could not see eye to eye, this vessel had a disastrous future, as did his Olympic dreams. Whatever the fate of all on board this vessel, Jonas knew he had to be prepared for war. They were now near the Lemurian shores for the second time and Captain Georgus seemed more indignant than ever. There were other Atlantean long boats following behind them toward Lemuria, but Captain Georgus was way in front. They secretly approached the shore on a destitute piece of Lemurian land. No one had seen them arrive because they sailed the long way around and kept out of sight. They used their time bending magic to quickly get to the shores without being seen, just as they had used this skill before. Then Georgus lead his warrior crew to shore. He seemed to know exactly where to head: to the Lemurian temples.

CHAPTER TWENTY-THREE

War is in the Air

Aurelia stood alone in the forest, knowing there was something awful brewing. She stood amongst the flowers reminding herself how to create healing herbs in case she had to help the wounded. She felt instinctively that yet another battle was upon them. Aurelia felt she would soon be using herbs and flowers to create a cure for sickness. This would benefit the people of Mu.

Aurelia smelled the herbs, testing each one, but her concentration was interrupted by shouts coming from one of the temples. She heard an unfamiliar booming voice. The name Georgus was mentioned.

'Georgus is here and is armed! Throw down your weapons in this temple - I beg of you!' Adama, the ruling priest of Lemuria bellowed.

Another man's voice boomed, 'No more talking!' He kept repeating, 'It is time for war!'

Aurelia hid behind the tree of wisdom and heard every word clearly.

'You are not superior to us! Fight me! I am Georgus of Atlantis! Fight me!'

Aurelia knew many secrets from the telling tree of wisdom, but this was different. Aurelia could hear a lot of voices shouting. Animosity filled the air. Hearing the clangs of swords and groans from warriors, Aurelia realised the Atlanteans came prepared for another battle with weapons and swords. They obviously wanted to fight. How did they sneak onto the lands again? She heard Adama trying to calm everyone down, to no avail. A brawl started and his shouts stopped no one. Aurelia could hear men being slain and did not know where to turn.

Even Adama had not seen this coming. Adama was so concerned with the sinking of Lemuria that he had not consulted his guides about another Atlantean invasion. Rochelle had not warned him either, meaning he was supposed to deal with it himself. Fighting broke out by the courts inside one of the main temple gates. More and more warriors joined in.

Aurelia really didn't know what to do. She could read the plants but not chaotic situations. Should she protect her family? Or stay listening at the city walls? Calmly, Aurelia listened to her intuition to find out what to do.

She ran! She wanted to get the children to safety and tell the women in the neighbourhood that a riot had broken out inside the main temple gates. Women started panicking as news spread to their husbands who speedily picked up weapons and joined in the fight for their motherland.

Aurelia wanted to stop the men. Aurelia felt fear at the wisdom tree, something didn't feel right. Aurelia knew however, that if she tried to stop them, her words would fall on deaf ears due to their desire for blood.

Aurelia felt a sudden surge of confidence rise within her and she ran to the market place. Aurelia cried, 'Women! Children! Follow me! I know a safe place!'

Surprisingly people did not hesitate. They were scared and needed a leader in that moment.

They all listened to the sorceress. Aurelia, her brother, many women and their children all ran into the forest that she knew so well. The others did not know the way but followed her.

Those following Aurelia were stricken with fear, so she calmed them by explaining about the crystal caves and how they would be hidden there. She told them that the caves had healing properties that would help any wounded they would find. Aurelia ran feeling like she was finally the leader she was born to be: a helper and a healer that people would respect and recognise. Whether they would all live or die, Aurelia did not know. Aurelia felt like her fate had already been decided for her. The sorceress wanted to try and hide as many people as possible from the war and potentially from the lethal waves that she heard so much about in the debates in the temples.

When the masses were safe in the caves, Aurelia told them all to stay calm. She informed them that she must go, she must try and help others and that she would be back soon. The young healer then kissed her brother and headed straight back through the forest to the temple gates. The masses that had followed her looked on in amazement at the beautiful pink and white crystals that adorned the caves as Aurelia fled.

Aurelia headed toward the temple, through the forest that she knew so well. She felt like a leader and she had things to say. She was no longer afraid. The battle had flooded onto the streets of Lemuria and the many of the beautiful temples looked destroyed. It was as if the destruction of the once powerful temples was a symbol: a symbol of defeat. Many priests were fighting, some priestesses remained, looking distraught. There seemed to be one common feeling amongst all - shock.

Aurelia fearlessly walked in a room full priestesses and everyone turned to her. It was her time to speak. As she stepped forward, the room was immediately silenced. She took centre stage in the icy cold stone room and no one moved a muscle. Everyone waited with anticipation for her to speak.

Aurelia pleaded, 'Please help us, my priestesses! Help your people! I know a secret place! I can take more innocent people to the crystal caves! Please help me take them there. No more death! Please, no more fighting!'

The priestess of the sea, Amara stepped forward, looking as if she knew Aurelia was going to say this.

Aurelia declared, 'The great war is here, that is clear. The fighting will continue and more deaths will be inevitable. The clash of opinions are too strong for either party to surrender. Each side has a different viewpoint which is never going to be understood by the other. The Atlanteans are all full of anger and emotion and will stop at nothing to tell us they will rule the continent their way. They will not learn from the Lemurians because they choose not to.

The gods will have no choice but to sink us. There is no other way. Inevitably, Atlantis will suffer the same fate, but not just yet, as they will have beautiful moments to come. Those that want to leave need to leave the beautiful continent of Mu now. Some will be too sad to leave this alluring, heavenly place. Yes, some may go to the caves and await their fate. Some will want to stay put, some will leave, some will start new generations on different continents.'

Amara nodded to Aurelia and telepathically told her that she would be supported in helping those who were going to hide out in the crystal caves.

Amara told her that everything she had said was correct and that the priestesses also believed the same thing.

Aurelia felt even more powerful. She left the room with added vigour and complete belief in herself. She ran as fast as the wind to the masses in the streets. Aurelia managed to immediately gather hundreds more Lemurians and they all followed her to the caves. They all listened to her! She told the masses the priestesses had sent her and they all listened.

She finally realised she had the gift of leadership.

****

Back in the priestesses' chambers Amara continued to address the other women after Aurelia had run out of the building, 'Do not panic my priestesses. We can all help. Yes, there is a war. Yes, some will be saved. Aurelia can now help to guard those in the hidden caves … ' She paused and looked to the floor. 'I do not know their fate'. She shook her head looking sad. Hundreds if not thousands of people were now heading for the secret caves for protection, were they going to live? She did not know.

There was a big pause as the priestesses looked on, worried.

Then Amara took a deep breath and continued: 'Someone will have to look after the special children who have magic powers beyond their comprehension. These children need to be protected. There are certain children who know more than we will ever know and therefore must be looked after. They are the leaders of the future'.

As Amara was speaking, she was looking straight at Princess Serafina.

Serafina was a typical looking Lemurian with long, wavy blonde hair. She was very thoughtful and had an ethereal look about her. She was always daydreaming and her imagination tended to run wild. Her heart was bigger than her whole being. She taught and educated children about the animals, the trees, the flowers, herbs and food. She also taught children about manifestation. Serafina educated the youngsters about many natural topics including the lay of the beautiful land of Mu. Serafina was not at all bothered by the war. This did not concern her. She was only interested in the welfare of the younger generation, the future leaders of Mu.

Everyone in the chambers turned to look at Serafina. Serafina always knew she had a calling and knew it had something to do with children. As a princess and the grandchild of an elder, she was well respected throughout the land of Mu. However, she had no political title. People would bow to Serafina when she walked past them. She had such a beautiful soul that she cared for everyone and everything. She would stop in her tracks to bless the flowers. If she saw an animal that looked distressed, she would stop and pray for the poor creature. She knew how to bring out the best in children by getting them to see their true, beautiful selves.

She genuinely wanted to help them. The princess believed that the children were the future and that the succeeding generations would be far smarter than them.

Serafina also believed in the power of crystals, like the Lemurian seed crystal and many more. She would often teach young children that crystals hold memories. Serafina would tell children that they could put knowledge inside a crystal for the future generations to find. Serafina knew that Lemuria wasn't always going to be their home, so she wanted others to learn about the motherland by feeling Lemuria through the crystals. Serafina taught children how to add the memory and how to bury the crystals in the earth.

When she was a little girl, Serafina would stare at the crystals and was obsessed with the beauty of each individual crystal when the light hit it. Different crystals made her feel a certain way. She learned that seed crystals had memories within them. She became obsessed with keeping records in crystals and was excited that one day a new race would find out about Lemuria and would be able to read her memories. The princess did not want the history of Mu to be lost and forgotten forever.

Serafina told the children that others would one day want to learn about Lemuria and Atlantis and how these two sacred, ancient, incredible continents were thriving with love and beauty. Serafina knew it was important to have a history that others could learn from.

Serafina stepped forward in the temple, heading toward the great ocean priestess Amara. She slowly lifted her head and stared directly into Amara's eyes.

Serafina spoke, 'I have always known that I am here for a reason. I am forever dutiful toward children. I would be honoured to look after the children during this transition. Whatever is my destiny matters not to me, but I will endeavor to keep the children safe during these changing tides'.

Serafina's mother and father came into the room halfway through the commotion. They were amazed and shocked. Serafina's parents were the King and Queen of the mainland. There were many different towns and villages within the spherical grid that made up the Lemurian continent. Serafina was well known throughout all the lands because of her family heritage. Her parents were well-respected within the communities. While the elders, priests and priestesses ruled, the King and Queen also had duties within the motherland.

Queen Aerlie spoke, 'How do I know my daughter will be safe? She is a free spirit and has a huge, giving heart. This is a big burden for someone of such innocence; someone so young. How do we know she will be looked after by the gods? Serafina may say she is put here for a reason, but I am not so sure. Serafina is my only daughter, my little girl and always will be in my eyes.'

The Queen had a way of distancing herself from the common folk. She had an icy stare she used on everybody and no one knew when the Queen was happy. The Queen had skills unbeknownst to the majority: soul connections. Queen Aerlie had the ability to see through each person's soul. The Queen could tell if a soul was happy and she knew what made each soul sing. The Queen was excellent at discerning the truth about each soul. She could tell if someone was with their true soul partner and how many lives each soul had previously had. Although she may have been distant and icy, the Queen was powerful, wise and all knowing. The King looked on in wonder, never saying much. He spoke slowly and carefully with a huge amount of control. He had a very deep, gravelly voice. It was the voice of an old wise soul.

King Gaileth reflected, 'Serafina knows her own mind. She may be a daydreamer with a big imagination. However, she has always had an inner sense of knowing. She just does not communicate that to others. She doesn't feel the need to communicate what her fate is. I knew she had a purpose the moment she was born, and that purpose would be with children. It seems like the time has come. However, do understand my wife's concerns about her safety as any parent would, especially the parent of a future Queen. Our son Joel is at sea and our daughter will soon be on a special mission across the oceans too; you can see our concern'.

Amara considered, 'It is the wish of the gods for Serafina to look after the magic children. The gods are aware that no one knows the children better than Serafina. This is her purpose. We can pray for the princess' safety and order some guards to watch over her and leave the rest in the hands of the gods.'

Serafina walked forward and bowed to her mother and father. The King put both of his hands on the dutiful princess' head to give a blessing. The Queen just stared at Serafina without an ounce of emotion on her face. The Queen felt deeply, yet hid this well.

****

There was no time left. People were running in all directions. Atlantean boats were arriving but there were many more in the distance. It was clear that some Lemurian and Atlantean boats at sea were sinking or on fire. The great Lemurian boat, the Criterion, and all on board including Roberto King of the Seas, were lost. Mothers were gathering their children and animals and heading for the secret caves they had heard whispers about. Men were getting ready to fight. Some felt the love of the land too much and stood still, awaiting their fate. If the Atlanteans didn't kill them, they awaited the great wave from the gods to engulf them. The love of the motherland was too strong for so many. They could not bear to think about leaving. They would rather sink, letting the true Lemurians be buried under the sea.

Princess Serafina noticed thunder and lightning engulfed the skies and a huge storm was upon

Lemuria. The prediction had begun. It was evident that the gods were not happy. There were cracks in the sky from the lightning, not dissimilar to the cracks in the Lemurian community. The lightning was visible as it struck the mountains from a distance. The waves seemed to get higher and higher. The waves looked like they would soon encapsulate the boats and all the rocks on the sides of the shore.

Amara, priestess of the ocean, had instructed the special children to follow Serafina and she had given the princess an important artefact: a crystal skull. This ancient rarity was a way for her to contact the elders and the gods in times of need. It was a shining, bright white and blue crystal skull. Serafina was scared to carry it, for she might drop it or someone might see it. She decided to keep it under her long blue cloak. The battle carried on in the distance. It was as if the people of Lemuria were used to the fighting and the killing now. Behind Serafina were children walking toward an unmanned shore. Some were alone as the parents could not be found and some were with their scared looking mothers.

Serafina was to guard these children with her life. These were called the 'indigo children': the children with special spiritual skills of the future. These gifted children were the chosen ones who would be ruling Lemuria in years to come. Wherever the Lemurians were moving too, these children would be instrumental in their future.

Christian, Serafina's soul mate, helped her onto the boat. She had said goodbye to her mother and father, but could not bear to say goodbye to her love. As she embraced him, she felt the same love for him as she did for her blessed land. Serafina couldn't believe she had to leave without him. She took one final look at the motherland and realised she did not know if she would ever see Lemuria again.

As she got on the boat, the fighting was getting closer to her and the children. Serafina could hear cries and screams. It was time for her to take the children away. The gods would decide where they were headed. She trusted, as she had no other option.

Serafina knew her mother and father would be absolutely fine, as they were also taking a boat to the new land with Adama, Zadiel, Serene and Amara. However, Serafina could not help but worry about them, and especially worry about Christian, her betrothed. Serafina knew to be selfless at this moment because she had nearly one hundred children to look after.

Serafina took a deep breath and held the crystal skull tightly.

Their boat finally left the shore, sailing away from the fighting. Serafina had an unbelievable sense of hope coming from within; they were going to be fine.

CHAPTER TWENTY-FOUR

Serafina's Story at Sea

Serafina was too scared to tell them she did not have any answers and did not know where they were going. Amara told her to follow the wisdom in the crystal skull. Serafina had an innate sense of knowing that Amara's words were correct. Serafina had a gift, the gift of knowing. Serafina may not have been as spiritually connected as Amara, but Serafina knew she had a gift. This gift was not only to discover the psychic ability within children, but also to guide others to their safety, to their soul's purpose and to love their true selves. She knew that with the help of the skull, the elders, the gods and her intuition, she could guide all of the children to safety. She looked up to the sky. The day had turned into night as the fighting continued. Serafina felt the crescent of the moon speaking to her: it said she should hold the crystal skull tightly.

As she looked at the dark night sky she saw an image in her head. A land! A new land! A land with people, boats, laughter, love and children!

Serafina asked, 'Show me skull, where is this land?'

The skull spelled out a word: Atlantis.

Serafina dropped the skull to the floor of the boat. She was to sail to Atlantis? But the war! The people disliked Lemurians! Why would she sail these children to their deaths? They were sailing the opposite way, to steer clear of any battles at sea! Were they to turn around? Did they have enough manifesting power away from Lemuria to get food and water?

The skull spelled again: Head to Atlantis. You will be safe.

CHAPTER TWENTY-FIVE

The Arduous Journey:

Serafina, the mothers and the children slept on the boat for three moons. They were disorientated with shock and worry. There had been enough food manifested so they were all strong and Serafina tried to keep up the morale of the children, the mothers and the naval officers by being her upbeat, loving self. She kept the skull a secret from all. This was her only source of instruction and her only point of hope.

Sea gulls appeared, meaning land was near. The long journey was over. Serafina should be relieved, but now she became even more anxious. What was to become of them now?

As Serafina looked to see the shores of Atlantis way off in the distance, she saw a glimpse of a beautiful green and blue tail. This was no ordinary tail; she knew this was a mermaid! The mermaid popped her head out of the sea and smiled, before quickly disappearing back to the depths. In that split second, Serafina felt as if the mermaid was giving her a message. It felt like a message of hope.

CHAPTER TWENTY-SIX

Lemurians on Atlantis Soil:

They arrived weary, hungry and thirsty. There had been a 'karmic contract' made up between the Lemurians and the people of Atlantis that certain Lemurian children would have a future in Atlantis. It was a common law that children could not be knowingly punished or held accountable for the battles of adults.

After the crystal skull informed Serafina to sail to Atlantis, she had spoken at length to the head priest Adama through the crystal skull. The counsel made the agreement with Atlantis that no one on Serafina's vessel would be hurt and the Lemurian children would be integrated with the people of Atlantis. Adama could not hide the doubt in his voice as he spoke to

Serafina through the skull, but they all knew to follow orders from the gods.

Serafina did not hear from Christian, her love, but was informed that he managed to escape the fighting and was on the boats heading to the new, secret land. This gave her relief that he would be okay.

Serafina felt very strange in a completely different land. It was as if her powers were dulled. It was her priority to help these amazing children in every way possible and to her, nothing else mattered.

****

As they took their first steps on this new land, they felt the war was over, even though it was fresh in their heads. Serafina lead the children from the boats and they were shown to their new living quarters. Serafina would never forget what she saw next. She saw hundreds of dead warriors, Lemurian and Atlantean. They were lined up as if they were sleeping peacefully on the floor and the soldiers were playing dead lying on their backs. However, this was no game. Serafina noticed some had their throats cut. The bloody after effect of the war was right in front of her and the children. The war might have been over but the horror of the aftermath was right in front of them. How would the children ever be able to forget that image?

****

As the Lemurians settled into their living and schooling quarters, Serafina tried to make things as normal for the children as possible. Although she missed her family, she was able to talk to them telepathically using the crystal skull for knowledge and information. However, she still felt very scared and alone.

The Atlanteans had been cordial to her but she couldn't help but notice how they distanced themselves from her. She had no other company outside of the classroom except her own thoughts. The pull of Lemuria was strong; she was completely homesick and categorically wanted to go back there. This was a crazed thought because none of them even knew if Lemuria was still there! It was terrifying to think that the motherland could have sunk beneath the waves by then. Plus, she knew that her journey with these children was not over.

Serafina lived in the school. She had about one hundred children growing up and learning beautifully. There were about twenty mothers with the children to help out. Serafina slept in quarters close by and was living a simple life. She knew only a few Atlanteans. There were other Lemurians there who decided to join Atlantis after the war, for they didn't have a choice. They needed a land to live on. So she sometimes sought the company of her own race but, due to her regal ways and her royal heritage, she was often left on her own.

There was an Atlantean gentleman who was regularly seen around Serafina named Andreas. He would help her carry things like food for the children and some educational materials that she needed. He mainly worked on the boats with other naval officers.

Andreas had a very kind heart. He knew they were from different cultures and would not be right for each other, but he could not help but have feelings for this big-hearted beauty. Serafina tried to distance herself from him but he never stopped being there for her. He didn't have the strength to stay away from her.

Serafina would normally walk down by the boats, feeling nothing but utter sadness for her family and her motherland. She missed Lemuria. Regardless of the fighting and war, she still wanted to go back home.

One day, Serafina was walking along the boats and some workers were courteous enough to greet her and say hello. Andreas gave her a hand on to one of the naval longboats and told her not to go down to the front of the vessel.

Andreas cautioned, 'Serafina don't go down to the front today. You will not like what you see. Just stay near me. You must promise me this.'

Serafina answered him, 'I promise. I have my duties to the children. I will stay here today. I have seen enough and I do not need to see any more destruction.'

Serafina quickly sent her wishes and her healing unto the sea. She sent her thoughts and prayers to her mother. She could hear glimmerings of psychic premonitions of those on the new lands.

Serafina's heart could feel what others felt. Her empathy was unprecedented. She tried to hide her tears as she realised how much she missed her loved ones and headed back to the school huts.

A little girl named Angela ran up to her crying. Serafina asked what was wrong and Angela just said, 'My daddy! My daddy!' and then ran out of the school huts down to the beach and across the boats. Serafina did not know what to do but she could not leave the little girl. She had to follow her and find her. Serafina told the children to stay in the classroom and went after Angela.

She called her name over and over, but she would not stop running. Angela had a blue ribbon in her hair and was wearing a white dress. Serafina got a glimpse of this blue ribbon flying through the wind, heading somewhere that felt dangerous.

Angela cried again, 'Daddy! Daddy!'

That was all Serafina could hear. She didn't know what was happening. Angela was always daydreaming. Sometimes, it was like she was watching a film of someone's life in her head. After she watched the film, she would come back into her human body. Angela would then tell the tales and stories for other people to sit and listen in wonder at how this incredible four-year-old had this ability to see such unbelievable predictions so clearly and in motion. Serafina wondered if this was just another day dream of Angela's or if it was a real premonition. Serafina quickly ran past all the vessels and headed to the front of the long boat she had been on before. Serafina saw the little girl sitting, crying and she could see a pair of feet. As she looked on she realised this was Angela's father, Roberto, the renowned Lemurian nicknamed the King of the Sea. He had been attacked at sea and his throat was cut.

The little girl was crying and crying at her father's feet. What a terrible sight for this poor four-year-old to see. Serafina slowly and carefully held the little girl from behind and just let her cry. She gave the comfort that the little girl needed. Angela's mother, Cleopatra had not crossed the sea with her daughter, so it was Serafina's task to love her like never before.

Serafina did not know what to do as the little one was crying uncontrollably. She knew someone was walking up behind her and sensed a kind presence. It was Andreas. He did not want Serafina to see any more of the monstrosity of death.

The princess stood quietly as she held the little one. She glanced to her right and caught sight of a blond, curly-haired boy's body lying on the ground. She recognised the soul and looked at the peaceful face. It was Joel her brother.

The realisation hit her hard: her brother, the prince, her only brother. It was as if she was struck by a dagger in the heart. Her mind went completely blank and she just stood there holding Angela in shock. What should she do?

She let go of Angela and gave the weeping girl to Andreas. Serafina ran to her brother and cried incessantly. The scene was somber. Now, there were two girls crying over men who had been killed during a pointless war. Serafina sobbed. Andreas then stood behind her, holding her to give her comfort while also holding Angela. The irony of the scene was astounding. An Atlantean naval officer was now giving comfort to Lemurians.

Serafina could not take this anymore. She was in a land where she was not fully accepted. She was miles away from her parents. Her one and only sibling, her caring, courageous brother, was dead. A four-year-old was crying her heart out over the death of her beloved father. There was only one thing that Serafina could do. She wiped away her tears. She knew she had to speak to the head priest himself, Adama.

Andreas said, 'Serafina, I told you not to come; this is no place for women. You must know that these are courageous soldiers. They will all be honoured. There is no war with them anymore. We all die and go to the same place, we all go back into the earth or we go to heaven. We are here to look after each other now. Let me look after you.'

Serafina held the little girl's hand and ran with her. They passed all the vessels. She didn't even notice the call of the ocean like she normally did. She had to get back to all the little ones. She had to save them and take them somewhere safe, somewhere else, somewhere that felt like home. Serafina no longer cared if there was not a clear, safe passage across the sea. This was the reason they had to come to Atlantis in the first place. No one wanted to risk the deaths of the little ones en-route to the new Lemuria. Serafina now decided that she was taking the children to the new lands, regardless. She could be here no more, the smell of death was ripe. How could she stay in a land that killed her brother? It was time to speak to the gods. The gods needed to ensure safe passage to the new lands. Enough was enough.

Serafina ran to the huts. She rummaged through the foliage next to her sleeping quarters to find her hidden weapon. Her parents had given her the crystal skull to use if she needed to contact them in case of emergencies. She had not used it on land because she was afraid that the Atlanteans would see it and take it from her. She looked around and saw no one. She grabbed the skull, hid it in her robes and entered the classroom with the little girl. She attended to her class and gave them an assignment using their third eye. While they were concentrating, she took Angela to the side. Angela sobbed as Serafina closed her eyes. She asked to see her own mother as she held the skull. Within a moment, the Queen's face was in Serafina's mind's eye.

The Queen spoke, 'We know about Prince Joel. We know about your brother. We are distraught. I am so sorry, Serafina, for how you found out. Your father has been keeping an eye on you from afar. It must have been terrible to see Joel that way.'

Serafina responded, 'Mother, this is no place for the children. This is no place for me. We are outcasts here. Only a few speak to us; they look at us as if we are vagabonds! Only today, one of my pupils saw her father,

Roberto, dead! She is sobbing uncontrollably as we speak. There is only one thing to do. I need to speak to Adama. I have to bring them home.'

Adama spoke then, 'I can see you, child. I'm with you in spirit. We knew this day would come. The gods have already allowed it. It will be difficult for you to get the children off Atlantis unseen. You must be careful so the Atlanteans do not follow. But now that we have found our way, it is safer for you to follow us. There was no way you could have brought the children here any earlier, as we did not know it was safe. This is no job for you alone. However, I know you Serafina. I know you live for the little ones. We have foreseen this. It will be difficult to get them out in secret. We must plan everything carefully.'

****

Days went by that felt like weeks. The plan had to be perfect in every way. The Atlanteans could not have a clue that the children were leaving. They might start asking questions about why the Lemurians were leaving and where were they to go? They could not risk the people of Atlantis following them to the new, secret lands and destroying them.

Serafina went on with her class normally, knowing well that when the sun was full, the boat would be waiting for her on the shore. She told the children that they were going down to the shore for an adventure.

They held hands two by two, mothers in tow, and they sang all the way down to the shore. She saw some sailors and smiled at them. She kept walking as if nothing was happening. At the very last boat, she could see a very tall person hiding in the boat - it was Adama. He was ready to take them to a new land.

They got away without anyone batting an eyelid. Who would be stupid enough to flee Atlantis in broad daylight?

Serafina felt safe with Adama and she was so pleased to no longer be in charge. She never really liked being the voice of authority.

As they sailed away, no-one really noticed them leaving nor did they care; the Atlanteans probably thought they were going for a short sail.

Although Serafina could feel eyes burning in the back of her head as the boat left the shore. She turned to look to the edge of the ocean and there was Andreas standing in the ocean as the waves lapped upon him. As the tide was going out, Serafina was leaving, for good. He looked at her with unrequited love. Andreas looked longingly at her with eyes full of tears, he knew he would not be seeing her again.

The children were very well behaved on the voyage. They ate the fruits that Serafina had collected. They sang songs, played with flowers and created rhymes and stories; they were content. The one person Serafina could not wait to see again was Christian, her beloved. She was so very in love with him and she knew they had a spark. She needed to set aside her personal feelings and do her duty to protect the children. But now that she had almost completed her mission, she could not wait to be in Christian's arms again.

Serafina spent a lot of her time singing with the children on the boat to make them happy. She kept her spirits high and kept her face full of smiles for the children. She knew that one or two of the little girls were exceptionally psychic and they were picking up on her nerves.

Even though Serafina was more than capable of looking after the children, she had always needed a push from her parents. She had a lot of insecurities. She had this feeling that she was not good enough to take care of these beautiful young beings that would shape the future.

She was one of the purest Lemurians - a princess, a healer and a helper of all young souls and all nature, yet so naive and so insecure. Her parents, through the voice in the crystal skull, gave her the encouragement she needed to get the children home safely. It was going to be a long journey, which scared her. The nights were long and cold but she absolutely knew it was her destiny to save these children.

The days seemed to get shorter and the nights became longer. As they followed the sunrise, the nights got colder. It was very dark on the boat and only the stars served as their light. Serafina would check that all the children were warm enough. They would huddle together to keep each other snug.

Serafina started to have thoughts about Christian, her soul mate. She did not know if he would be glad to see her or annoyed at her selfless behaviour. He always wanted to protect her. She looked out on the ocean and asked for the dolphins and the mermaids to come forward. Sometimes they would and she would look at them, admiring the freedom they had in their lives. She would often wish she had their liberty. However, she knew she had too much of a sense of duty to go off and play with them.

One particular mermaid would often come up to the boat to have a glimpse of them all. It was the very same one she saw as they arrived in Atlantis. The mermaid had very grey eyes and long white-grey hair. She looked a little sad now, as if she could feel Serafina's pain. However, she seemed to stare in a knowing way, which was comforting. Serafina would just look at her. They both had this sense of childlike purity that connected them on some level. As quickly as the mermaid appeared, she flashed her tail and was gone.

The children were getting weary, tired, hungry and bored of the same songs over and over again. However, something was telling Serafina to continue on with the journey. She knew they were nearly there. Adama looked at her knowingly; they must be close to land.

Serafina was hungry, too, and it started getting colder. There were no signs of the mermaid now and very little fish life for them to eat. She was manifesting her food as much as she could. Both Adama and Serafina could not feel the magic from Lemuria anymore, so alchemy became more difficult even for Adama. Serafina took it for granted that the energy in the land of Mu would be everywhere, yet she found manifesting much more difficult. There was a dark, heavy energy around her. She could feel the call from the ocean priestess, Amara, and she knew she was getting closer to her fellow Lemurians. However, she struggled to get any sense of feeling from her family and her friends.

The children started laughing, joking and giggling again after a prayer to the gods. Serafina noticed that the lower energies that seemed to be engulfing the boat did not have a direct effect on the children like it did on her and Adama. She started to notice energy and how it affected people in different ways. She realised the more innocent a person is, the easier it is to rise above the darkness.

It was very hard for her to do magic whenever she was in a negative state. She would get almost depressed and this caused her to see her premonitions only vaguely. She started to realise how different everything was without her beloved land. Isn't it funny how you don't realise how much you love something until you lose it?

'Fina! Fina!' Angela called. She was jumping up and down pointing at some beautiful, white parrots flying around, birds that Serafina had not seen before. Serafina was sure they were not birds of the sea. It was as if the beauty of the white birds above them was a gift from god. The white feathered creatures symbolised peace to Serafina. She knew she was coming home and peace was in the air. Adama now knew land must be close.

The crystal skull started heating up. Serafina had been in such a trance that she didn't even notice the crystal skull all morning. Serafina didn't even realise it was morning already. The journey had become so long it was as if the days and nights had all melted into one. Serafina could only liken this to staring at the horizon, not knowing where the ocean ended and the sky began.

She touched the crystal skull and felt Adama's warm energy. 'We are almost here', he said.

All the children started to awaken from their slumber because of Angela's cries. Dolphins appeared, jumping out of the water. It almost felt like the dolphins were helping the boat move faster. Serafina slowly realised she needed to get excited and happy to get her magic back. The boat would never have gone this fast without the help of the dolphins that were now trailing them. Serafina realised she needed to be in an excited state for her magic to come back. She just needed to get the formula right all the time to create magic. This formula seemed to be the feeling of excitement and happiness.

CHAPTER TWENTY-SEVEN

The Motherland Lemuria

The flames in the forest were dulling due to the rains and storms. Damien looked on at Lemuria, hardly recognising his motherland. As the torrent of rainfall put out the fires he knew he must follow Mother Earth's lead and dampen the war.

Damien cried, 'People, we must stop the fighting! Look at Mother Earth's fury! It is clear the gods are not happy with us! The waves will soon engulf this land. Just look!'
Damien pointed to the one-hundred-foot-high waves in the distance. The people of Atlantis and Lemuria looked out to sea and gasped in horror.

'We must stop!' said Damen as he boldly took a sword from an Atlantean warrior and threw it to the floor in anger.

Damien carried on, 'We must leave this land in peace! We knew this time would come, even if we did not want believe it. There is nothing we can do. Mother Earth has spoken. The gods are talking to us now. We must stop fighting with Atlantis and then I promise you they will stop fighting, too.' Damien could not hold back the tears anymore and his once booming warrior voice was reduced to that of a child. He looked at his rivals, straight in their eyes. Looking through their souls.

He concluded, 'The Atlanteans will follow our lead. They may think we are the weaker race. However, strength comes from love. Let's show them our love. Let the love shine through. Stop fighting and put down your weapons. Come sit with me and sing to the gods right now.'

Damien couldn't believe what he was saying. He was once a fighter, bred for war. Once upon a time he could not wait to fight for his country and for his people. Yet now he was letting a guardian angel channel through him telling others to stop fighting with Atlantis.

Adama had asked Damien to go to the new lands and to help lead the people there, but Damien wanted to stay. He knew there would be masses of people that would not leave the motherland and they needed a leader, a leader with an angelic guide. He knew his duties.

The moment Damien stopped talking, the waves started talking for him. There was a rumble out to sea. A wave at least one thousand feet high was seen in the distance heading towards the shore. It was a long way off and it would be a few minutes before it would hit them, before life as they knew it would be gone.

What to do in the last few moments of your life? They all knew in that instant that Mother Earth was responding directly to the war. The rumble of the enormous wave felt like a message from Mother Earth, it was as if she was saying, 'You didn't listen.'

Damien knew time was running out and desperately needed to talk to Rochelle and looked up to the sky to find her. He knew that not all Lemurians could see her, but he wanted as many as possible to see her. He wanted them to know that he was channeling from a higher source, so that they would continue to listen to him and they could all end their lives with peace and not war.

Rochelle appeared behind Damien. Rochelle put her hands on Damien's shoulders, and with that, she became a pure white figure for all to see. All the crowds of Lemurians were taken aback and were looking on in wonder. They could see this white figure with wings and knew they were looking at an angelic being. Rochelle was clearly not a Lemurian. Rochelle held onto Damien as if she was gaining power from gripping on to him. As a few seconds passed, Rochelle's white, sheer image became a much more solid vision. She became human-like. Huge, white-feathered wings then spread out from her back. She was letting people know she was there but she was from a different realm: heaven.

The Lemurians were now seated on the ground thanks to Damien's command. Fighters from both continents were seen in the distance dropping their weapons and heading toward them. Mainly these were people from Atlantis. They gawped in wonder as they realised angels were real. This was truly a miraculous moment on the motherland. Captain Georgus and head crew member, Yonassis, from Atlantis were still alive and still battling on Lemurian soil. However, they soon stopped in their midst. Georgus threw down his sword. He knew that seeing an angel was a sign from the gods. Georgus and Yonassis went over to the crowds sitting calmly in circles on the very soil of the motherland they had previously wanted to destroy. They joined seated warriors without hesitation. Other Atlanteans followed Georgus' lead. Everyone sat down and was looking up at the beautiful, white-feathered angel. This was a spectacular view that no one had ever seen before and would never see again.

The view of the menacing waves was now obstructed by the sighting of the beauty of an angel.

They knew that seeing an angel would happen only once in a lifetime. The Atlanteans took this as a sign: the gods wanted them to stop the war.

Rochelle flew around trying to touch as many people from Atlantis as possible. She wanted to unite the masses. Some were bloody from the fight. Some were exhausted and some were in pain. However, everyone seemed to put their physical problems aside as they watched this alluring spectacle.

Damien felt the inner contentment rise within him. He spoke, 'The waves are coming; the waters will rise. Let us be as one. Let us not leave these lands with any anger or any more bloodshed. Let Lemurian soil be filled with our love. Let the future generations find Lemuria beneath the sea and let them feel the love here. Let future races discover positive, loving memories of our land. We will be buried with a love of our land.'

Damien pulled out a crystal from his pockets, saying, 'Put your loving thoughts, memories and healing into your seed crystals and bury them into the land.'

Again, Damien could not believe what he was saying. The man who once wanted to win the war was now telling people to put loving thoughts into crystals? Devastating waves would soon envelope the entire continent and they were sitting on the floor? Where was this coming from? He could not believe that the hordes of bloodied people in front of him were listening.

243

Some decided to bury their chains, necklaces, crystals and rings into the land. These artefacts were filled with love and buried, waiting for other species to find the lost memories of Lemuria.

****

Aurelia had a premonition to come out from hiding in the crystal caves. She had taken hundreds of children, mothers, the wounded and the elderly to the caves with her and now they followed her again. She carried flowers, plants and herbs, Aurelia had been using them to help the wounded. She knew her purpose was to help heal any sick or injured people after the fighting. Aurelia absolutely knew it was time to come out of hiding. The caves had given her followers an innate sense of calm. Some decided not to go with her and wanted to stay in the comfort and security of the caves. She left some of the mothers with their playing children with love and kindness yet also with a sadness in her heart. Aurelia did not know if she would ever see them again.

As she led the survivors to the shore, she was expecting to see a bloody mess. Instead, she heard mighty warriors humming the gods' song. She followed the beautiful sound. Aurelia saw Damien and, without a word, embraced him. They did not know each other, but she instinctively felt that they had both been instrumental in saving their people.

Aurelia knew it was time for love and peace, not war. She walked around the outer circle of seated warriors, offering love and healing to those in need. The elderly, women and children came to sit and hold hands with fellow Lemurians and the Atlantean troops. Aurelia seated herself next to Damien and, holding his hand, she gave him healing from her heart. Damien felt the pure love coming from her and thanked her with an embrace. The embrace seemed significant to Damien. Signifying that the old Lemuria ways had returned. Pure love reigned again.

Damien watched as the waves got closer. Damien knew these were his last moments on his precious continent. The remaining crowds held hands to create an unbreakable healing circle. Rochelle added her energy to the healing whilst flying in spirals. They sang the song of Lemuria and they sang to the gods. The remaining Lemurians that could not bear to leave the motherland sang in loving harmony to the gods and sang in gratitude for the time they had on their motherland. Even those from Atlantis were singing. Damien, with his masses, and Aurelia, with the children and the others from the crystal caves, were sitting in ever decreasing circles, feeling the healing energy rising up to the stars. They now needed to put all of this beautiful loving energy into the earth.

Rochelle, Damien and Aurelia asked for the energy they had created to go into the earth of Lemuria. They wanted to leave a happy, loving feeling in Lemuria. Aurelia and her crowds from the caves had also left thousands of Lemurian crystals buried in the land. These crystals held memories of the sacred years they had on their beloved Mu. No one in the circles ever wanted to leave the land again. They were happy to go down with the waves. The colossal amount of love and healing that surrounded them ensured that they did not want to be anywhere else. Jonas, the rower from Atlantis, sat in the outer circle holding hands with Charlie, Damien's good friend from Lemuria. It was as if they were lifelong friends.

Thesis, the head of the Lemurian warriors, was crying with love as he sang to his gods. It was as if the healing energy of Lemuria was so strong, no-one cared about the war anymore. They were all happy for this life to end. They knew their souls would continue. Everyone looked at each other with love and care. The people from Atlantis sat among the Lemurians and, at that moment, it became clear that they were united as one.

Water slowly started to rise as some of the waves crashed on to the shore. Damien knew it was time. He knew it was his fate to learn of his powerful, spiritual gifts and to use his gifts for good. Damien knew it was right to rise above battling others and killing. He knew he could lead a peaceful protest and was proud that he had managed to get hundreds of people to sit with him while the waves destroyed their land. Sitting with both friend and foe, Damien felt his life was complete; what more could he ask for?

Damien could hardly believe they had all followed him, but they did. The masses believed in Damien and that was good enough for him.

Damien knew he would die for his motherland and that was his choice: to stay and to die with Lemuria. He felt like he was part of Lemuria and could not live anywhere else. It seemed that many shared his love for Lemuria. He looked at Rochelle, who was now flying above the crowds creating healing energy, and he smiled at her with complete love. He thought of his brother Petrius, his father, his whole family and he made peace with himself. The waves were about to engulf the land. He shouted thanks to the gods and to Rochelle and, with that, a monster wave could be seen in the distance, a wave no continent could endure. His final moments were spent smiling at his beloved Rochelle with his beautiful, blue eyes, feeling the love from the motherland beneath him.

CHAPTER TWENTY-EIGHT

The welcome given to Serafina upon her arrival was immense. Parents were immediately reunited with the indigo children. Sobs of joy could be heard throughout the new land, which was to be named Telos. Christian was there with his arms open for his love, Serafina. Serafina's parents, the King and Queen, were in full regal robes to welcome her. It became obvious that a ceremonial welcome was the only way Serafina would be greeted. Fifteen thousand Lemurians travelled to Telos safely. Thousands of them clapped and sang to honour and welcome Serafina.

Serafina was just as dutiful and humble as ever. She knew she had to save the children, so she did not see herself as a hero. It was her fate. Serafina wanted to look around her new home, but the celebration had already started. The last thing she wanted was a ceremony. However, she accepted graciously. The children were taken in blankets to their new homes. Then, the masses sat in front of crackling fires to watch the ceremony in the warmth. Serafina was cold, tired and hungry but was whisked away by her mother to dress in official robes for her formal ceremony. Serafina took a quick look at the mountainous surroundings, noticed the cold air and the change in frequency. She wondered if her psychic ability would ever return. Her mother took her hand solemnly and walked her up to their home, waving to the masses all the while.

Queen Aerlie enjoyed her finery, so Serafina knew the palace would be spacious and elegant. They walked into a cave on the side of a mountain and were taken to a beautiful land of green, with space and lakes and magical energy. They were surrounded by mountain goats, sheep and horses. Serafina suddenly felt at home. The Palace was built within the mountainous terrain. It was the most stunning work of art she had ever seen. Serafina climbed the stairs to the highest point of their new home and was shown to her room. The view of the city was exceptional from this height. Serafina had always enjoyed being up high and being in the mountains. She knew she'd be happy here. Her mother walked in her room and Serafina bowed to her and kept silent.

The Queen said, 'Here are your robes. You are going to be Queen of Telos. You must tell everyone that living here will be the best thing for them. They will all listen to you because you are a hero.'

Serafina knew she was not a hero and did not want to convince anyone of anything. However, she bowed her head in silence.

The Queen continued, 'This blue gown was made especially for you. We have worked day and night so we could give you the welcome you deserved. I hope that you will enjoy this ceremony. You and Christian will be crowned the King and Queen of Telos tonight. After the feast, a boar will be slaughtered in your honour. You are to kiss your father's hand after the slaughter.'

Serafina kept quiet and bowed in agreement, knowing nothing but duty. Serafina would be sharing her life with Christian and couldn't be more pleased. She silently thanked the gods for Christian. She was grateful for her teachings and the children. She missed Lemuria, but she knew it would be wrong to bring this up. Her servants brought the gold-threaded robes and she got dressed for the ceremony.

Serafina asked, 'May I have a moment with mother?' Her ladies in waiting bowed and left the chambers. Her mother was staring at her with pride and joy, but also worried about what her daughter was about to say.

Serafina began, 'Mother, am I doing the right thing? I have been through so much. I spent time in Atlantis feeling like an outsider and I couldn't wait to get home. But now that I'm here, I don't feel like I deserve the attention or the grandeur. In all honesty, all I want is to look after the children and heal them. I know Christian is a good man and my soul mate. I do know that! I am grateful for him and longed for him on the cold nights on the boat. But is this right for me? To be Queen? To be waited on? It feels so wrong. What will happen to you and father?'

Serafina turned to find her father standing in the doorway. He had heard everything she said. Her mother and father walked to each other and stood before her.

The King said, 'Serafina, we know you and we knew you would feel this. You are but a humble girl. You never wanted riches or finery. You are a true Lemurian. You must understand that being a queen does not make you better than anyone else, it just makes you dutiful. It gives you a voice for the people and the children. You were given this role by the gods because of your kind nature and your leadership qualities. Your selfless demeanor means you will be a great leader, a leader of the people. With Christian by your side as a remarkable warrior, you will guide the people to happiness and tranquility here in Telos, the new Lemuria.'

Her mother stepped forward, looking agitated. She joined in, 'You are a remarkable gift from the gods, Serafina. With the help of the other rulers such as Adama, Zadiel, Serene and Amara, you can create the new Lemuria. Let us retire in peace while your younger energy takes over these new lands. Please do not think you are merely to be waited on wearing finery, as this was never the case. The gods gifted you to us and we are grateful every day for our gift. You are a special being, Serafina, and you are made for great things.'

The Queen glanced around the stone room to ensure privacy and looked curiously to her husband before addressing her daughter, 'It is time. Serafina, the gods have another mission for you; a mission that involves helping other, newer humans on earth, people that will not have the powers we do, a race that will not understand love the way we do. You can teach them. They are not born yet, but they will be soon enough and they will live close by to us but will not see us. This will involve time travel to meet other humans. Rochelle will be with you as you meet humans and help them understand what Lemuria is and who we are.'

Serafina was puzzled, 'But Rochelle is not in Telos. She stayed and went down with the waves in Lemuria.'

The Queen replied, 'Oh Serafina, angels cannot die. They are eternal. Yes, Rochelle helped those that would not leave Lemuria but trust me, she lives on and will be back for your next mission. The humans are in need of our help, Serafina, and you are the chosen one to help them live as if heaven were upon earth.

Serafina, go and get married, love Christian. Keep supporting Telos but know you are about to embark on the biggest mission of your life. This is not the end for you.'

Serafina gazed out of her windows at the landscape of Telos. She mulled over this proposal for what seemed like an eternity. She felt someone was by her side as she was pondering her future; it was Rochelle! She was already back! Rochelle was smiling at her. The feeling Rochelle was giving her was that all would be well. Serafina started to smile broadly and went to hug her parents. The maids were called back in. Her veil was placed on her head and her mother left to take her place at the front of the vast ceremony.

The King said, 'Shall we?' He looked at Serafina with loving and kind eyes. Serafina stepped forward to take her father's arm.

The trumpets were playing and the crowds became still. It was time. Serafina's new life was about to start and she could not wait to be married, to lead her people with love and to find out what these new humans on unknown lands were like.

The ceremony was beautiful and perfect. It was hosted by Adama, whose voice carried over the masses in a soft and gentle way.

Serafina was honoured for saving the children and then she was crowned. Christian was crowned, too, as her beloved spouse. Their reign began. Serafina's mother was so thrilled and happy that her daughter would reign in Telos under the command of Adama. The royals all looked pleased.

As Adama finished his speech, he said a prayer for all those lost in Lemuria. He mentioned Damien, the brave warrior who gave his life to help others and regained peace on Lemuria in his final moments upon the earth. The masses were silent as they honoured the dead, buried beneath the waves.

After they had prayed, Christian gazed at Serafina in awe. He was so happy to be by her side. Serafina rose unexpectedly. Adama bowed to her, looking at her with a knowing gaze. Amara looked encouragingly on at Serafina, always knowing ahead of time what would happen next. Amara did not look surprised.

Serafina addressed them, 'In my new role as the Queen of Telos, I want all of you to know that I will do my utmost to keep you safe. I will protect all my fellow Lemurians. I will search this new land for new ways of living. I will ensure we are not harmed. I surrender myself to Adama. Priest Adama, use me as you will to help our people survive in this new world. Let me surrender my soul over to you so you can use me at your will. Let me help you serve the good people of Telos.'

As usual, Serafina was dutiful and humble. The masses cheered for her. They could see she was selfless and pure hearted. They looked forward to her reign. Adama bowed to Serafina then took her hand and raised it to the masses. The biggest cheer ever heard throughout all of Lemuria was heard in the mountains that day - a cheer of pure love. A new Lemuria was born.

ABOUT THE AUTHOR

Tiffany Wardle is a global TV psychic and author from the UK. Tiffany Wardle spent five years working on Psychic TV, the largest psychic show in Europe. Tiffany has also previously hosted an angel radio show and was the owner of the well-known publication 'Angels Magazine'. Tiffany now travels the world to see clients and also to complete research about spiritual topics.

Tiffany Wardle has written four bestselling books so far. Topics include psychic abilities, energy centres on the body and she has also written two books about Lemuria - the age before Atlantis.

Tiffany has travelled the globe looking for research on Atlantis and Lemuria and she has collated her findings in her last two books. Tiffany Wardle is an expert on Lemuria and Atlantis and is now also a Lemurian healing teacher.

Lemurian healing is said to be 10 times as powerful as Reiki and is also a way to self-heal and also send distant healing to others.

As a psychic and a spiritual teacher, Tiffany has many well-known clients around the globe: some are royalty and some people just like you and me. Tiffany's more recent work has lent her to become a spiritual teacher as well as seeing clients on a one on one basis.

Tiffany's latest work 'Lemuria - The Buried Truth' is available worldwide.

Made in United States
Orlando, FL
21 May 2022

18048681R00146